D0369258

Restoring Economic Equilibrium

Human Capital in the Modernizing Economy

THEODORE W. SCHULTZ

Basil Blackwell

Copyright © Theodore W. Schultz 1990

First published 1990

Basil Blackwell, Inc.
3 Cambridge Center
Cambridge, Massachusetts 02142, USA

Basil Blackwell Ltd
108 Cowley Road, Oxford OX4 1JF, UK

Library of Congress Cataloging in Publication Data
Schultz, Theodore William, 1902–
  Restoring economic equilibrium: human capital in the modernizing economy/Theodore W. Schultz.
    p. cm.
  Includes bibliographical references.
  ISBN 1–55786–081–5
      1. Economic development. 2. Economic policy. 3. Equilibrium (Economics). 4. Income. 5. Entrepreneurship.   I. Title.
HD75.S38 1990
339–dc20   89–18621
                                                                        CIP

British Library Cataloguing in Publication Data
A CIP catalogue record for this book is available from the British Library.

Typeset in 10½ on 13pt Sabon by
Wearside Tradespools, Fulwell, Sunderland
Printed in Great Britain by
Billing & Sons Ltd., Worcester

Contents

Preface

In this book I am concerned about the origins, existences, and consequences of economic disequilibria that occur during the process of modernization. I treat such disequilibria as economic events. I see them as occurring at uneven rates. Even though the modernizing process has favorable income effects, disequilibria nevertheless occur. Some entail shocks usually accompanied by adverse income effects for some economic agents. My analysis concentrates on what these agents do to restore equilibrium. The critical issue is what determines the efficiency and success of families and individuals in restoring equilibrium in their economic domain. For evidence I draw mainly on studies pertaining to economic modernization of the last 40 years, the period since the Second World War.

I doubt that it is possible to obtain the increases in income to be had from economic modernization and not incur disequilibria. This class of disequilibria cannot be prevented by either a centralized Gosplan economy or an open competitive economy without loss of some income. Any economy that is beset with disequilibria is to some extent in a state of disorder. It may be true that the more rapid the pace and the greater the achievements of the modernization process, the greater the extent of the disorder within the economy.

It is not my intention to abandon equilibrium theory. It is all too easy to drift into the rocks of the irrelevance of equilibrium economics or to become fascinated by the subtlety and apparent analytical power of growth models, a dangerous course between Scylla and Charybdis for economists.

It is my contention that theory should be extended to treat the phenomenon of increases in income that originate out of the modernizing process. The required theory would seek to explain the sources of the increases in income. These sources are the results of human endeavors. The class of disequilibria that occur during this process are not immune to human endeavors to restore equilibrium. What people do under these circumstances is not routine or repetitive. The modernization process is not automated. People are not robots. As modernization occurs no law, policy, or rhetoric can keep such disequilibria from occurring. It is up to human agents to deal with these disequilibria. What they do is *entrepreneurship*, whether it is done by people in their private domain or by officials in the public domain. At that point the analytics concentrates on entrepreneurs, with special emphasis on their human capital, that serves them in restoring equilibrium.

My critique of economic development policies and growth models owes much to the Ph.D. research of graduate students, and to the discussions that their research entailed. My learning from graduate students began back when some of my colleagues were doing their first research: D. Gale Johnson, George Tolley, Lester Telser, Arnold Harberger, Larry Sjaastad, Gary Becker, and Sherwin Rosen.

Other graduates who also have become established as economists have influenced my thinking during their graduate years and by what they have achieved since then. It is a long list: Walton Anderson, Nicolas Ardito-Barletta, Frank Backmura, Marto Ballesteros, Richard Barichello, Charles Berry, James Berry, Charles Bishop, Basudeb Biswas, Guy Black, Leo Blakley, Gladstone Bonnick, David Boyne, Lawrence Brainard, Michael Brennan, Keith Campbell, Martin Carnoy, Jose Carvalho, Tarsicio Castaneda, Paulo de Castro, Roger

Chisholm, William Cook, Mario Corbo, Manuel Cordomi, George Coutsoumaris, John Dawson, Gilbert Dementis, Dennis DeTray, Richard Dowell, John Edwards, Robert Evenson, Robert Fearn, Lyle Fettig, Robert Firch, Walter Fisher, John Floyd, Ernesto Fontaine, Louis Fourt, Andrew Frank, Bruce Gardner, Delworth Gardner, Harry Gilman, Micha Gisser, Milton Glick, Louis Goreux, Zvi Griliches, Amyra Grossbard, Yehuda Grumfeld, Robert Gustafson, Joel Guttman, Harold Halcrow, Giora Hanoch, Vaughan Hastings, Reed Hertford, John Hildebrand, Pete Hill, Roger Hitchner, Irving Hoch, Dale Hoover, Wallace Huffman, Rufus Hughes, Leroy Hushak, Glenn Johnson, Paul Johnson, Ethel Jones, Michael Keeley, Yoav Kislev, Dale Knight, Raj Krishna, Daniel Landau, Carlos Langoni, John Letiche, Millard Long, Kenneth Lyon, Frank Maier, Indra Makhija, Sarma Mallampally, Mahar Mangahas, Arthur Mosher, Marc Nerlove, Wallace Ogg, Walter Oi, Lawrence Olson, Keijiro Otsuka, Ross Parish, Donald Parsons, Evertt Peterson, Willes Peterson, Todd Petzel, Clayne Pope, Hans Popp, George Psacharopoulos, Musunuru Rao, Assaf Razin, Lucio Reca, Joseph Reid, Edward Renshaw, Vernon Ruttan, Ezra Sadan, Gian Sahota, Edward Schuh, Aba Schwartz, Stanley Seaver, Marcelo Selowsky, Salem Sethuramen, Ralph Shlomowitz, Seymour Smidt, James Smith, Larry Smith, Lewis Solmon, Richard Steckel, Vasant Sukhatme, Daniel Summer, James Thompson, Procter Thompson, Lalgudi Venkataramanan, Dudley Wallace, Finis Welch, Clifton Wharton, Anne Williams, Robert Wolfson, Chung Ming Wong, Raul Yver, Juan Zapata, and Morton Zeman.

My debt to the most recent graduate students includes David Abler, John Antel, Yuko Arayama, Andrew Barkley, James Baumgardner, Karen Brooks, George Catsiapis, Miguel Gomez, Daniel Gros, Tariq Husain, Sheldon Kimmel, Justin Lin, Anita Mahesh, Tracy Miller, David Mitch, Kevin Murphy, John Nash, James Oehmke, Cesar Ramierz-Rojas,

Paul Romer, Claudio Sapelli, Maurice Schift, James Wen, and Yue-Chin Wong.

I am especially indebted to Gary Becker, Mary Jean Bowman, Milton Friedman, James Heckman, Bert Hoselitz, John Letiche, Robert Lucas, Sherwin Rosen, T. Paul Schultz, George Stigler, and Lester Telser for helpful suggestions on various chapters.

I deeply appreciate the contributions of three very special persons: my book benefited much from the rich editorial experience in economics of Elizabeth Johnson. Margaret Schultz spotted and corrected language ambiguities and literary weaknesses. Highly skilled Kathy Glover, in addition to her many secretarial tasks, stayed abreast of the many on-going revisions, and redid them, as if doing so were a pleasure.

Theodore W. Schultz

1

Introduction

The main purpose of this study is to improve our understanding of the process of economic modernization with primary attention to increases in income and to disequilibria that are consequences of this process.[1] These disequilibria are of a particular type.

Whatever the type, economic disequilibria are troublesome. Although they have observable economic attributes, it is usually assumed that they have a strong tendency to disappear, or they are unimportant, or they are abnormal entities. They are omitted from the core of economic theory. Omitting them simplifies the theory. But for lack of theory and evidence, all too little is known about the origins, existences, and processes of restoring equilibrium. *Ad hoc* theories will not suffice. The question arises whether equilibrium theory can be extended to treat and analyze such disequilibria. I take comfort, as I have elsewhere, from Hicks's[2] preface to *Capital and Growth* where he comments on a theory of economic growth that can be defended in every respect. He states: "I do not think there is such a theory; I doubt if there can be. The phenomena that are presented by a developing (changing) economy are immensely complex; any theory about them is bound to simplify.... There is no known approach which is not based upon omissions, omissions that can easily prove to be of critical importance."

This study will concentrate on three such omissions in growth theory which are of critical importance: (a) *specialization* as a key to most modern increases in income; (b) *disequilibria* as increases in income are realized from advances in technology, from the proliferation of human capital, and from other sources; and (c) *entrepreneurs* as agents in restoring equilibrium.

1 Income from Specialization

The part of *The Wealth of Nations* on the division of labor limited by extent of the market continues to be an important analytical component of economics. Extraordinary specialization has come to characterize modern high income economics. If we knew the economics of this vast specialization, we would know much of the economics that matters in achieving increases in income. In international trade, identically endowed countries have incentives to specialize and trade. Identically endowed individuals also have incentives to specialize in their skills and trade. Such income implications of specialization are a part of this inquiry.

Advances in technology are income increasing,[3] which consequently enhance specialization. It will become evident that advances in technology are man-made. New and better technologies are not free. In most high income countries there exists a substantial sector that specializes in the production of knowledge and on the utilization of parts of that knowledge in specialized organized research to develop technologies that are income increasing. We have learned that organized research is costly, that the results of technologically oriented research, time and again, turn out to be economic failures and some research ventures entail large investments over many years. Despite such failures and large costly ventures, advances in technology are a major source of additional income. Hybrid corn in the United States and the high yielding wheats in India are dramatic economic success stories.

The production of knowledge has become highly specialized; to wit, plant genetics has reached the stage that the creation of higher yielding crop varieties has become a highly skilled production process, tailored to the sunlight, temperature, rainfall, and the texture and acidity of the soil. Plant breeders also alter the required planting, cultivation, and harvesting so that the crop can be more readily mechanized. We observe that a symbiotic relationship develops among geneticists, chemists, plant breeders and soil scientists in research laboratories and in experiment stations, including engineers and technicians in factories producing farm machinery and other agricultural inputs. This research process entails a wide array of highly specialized human capital to create technologies that prove to be superior to those that exist. Increases in income derived from advances in technology in turn further enhance the income possibilities from more specialization.

Growth models either omit or underrate the increases in income from investments in human capital. The proliferation of the quality and quantity of human capital has become a major source of additional income. In this study we hold fast to specialized human capital. We look for spill-over effects from one person to another. Are people at each skill level more productive in high human capital environments? On this issue our hypothesis is that human capital enhances the productivity of both labor and capital. As in the case of technology, increases in income derived from human capital in turn further enhance the income-producing possibilities from more specialization.

2 Disequilibria from Modernization

It has become an art to conceal economic disequilibria that occur as a consequence of modern increases in income. The art of concealment is evident in growth models. Changes in economic conditions, be they technological or changes in specialized human capital, and whether or not they occur abruptly, are in general neglected in economics. Schumpeter's approach to economic development is a notable exception.

One part of the art of bypassing the disequilibria problems is to rely on a *tendency assumption* based on the proposition that there is such a tendency toward equilibrium, and that it suffices. Another part is to transform each actual disequilibrium into a hypothetical equilibrium by means of concepts of information and transaction costs, of subjective risk, and of expectations. Regardless of what may be learned from this approach, it avoids the problems of restoring equilibrium.

3 Entrepreneurs Restoring Equilibrium

Most of the literature in economics either neglects small entrepreneurs or treats them as if they were a burden on economic modernization. Even Schumpeter overlooked small entrepreneurs. Economic successes in agriculture during recent decades throughout much of the world have been achieved, in large measure, by small farmers. Large government farms have failed. Small-farm micro data have become abundant. Most of the empirical evidence presented in this study entails micro economics.

The disequilibria caused by economic modernization signal income-increasing processes, whereas builders of growth models appear to abhor such disequilibria as Nature abhors a vacuum. We need to be on guard inasmuch as "economic growth" is a biological metaphor that connotes a process that is steady, balanced, and orderly. What we need instead is a concept of income-increasing processes that are not burdened by biological connotations.

Historical perspectives of economic thought are useful in evaluating economic ideas and concepts. The process of modernization, driven to produce more income to attain preferred rising standards of living, is more closely akin to the classical idea of economic progress than it is to that of economic growth models.

Contrary to the long view of Ricardo, still held by most economists, farm land rent declines as a fraction of national income. It is one of the important consequences of economic modernization. The age old public choice tensions between economics and politics change as the political influence of landlords declines. Another major consequence originates out of the increases in the quality of the labor force, the rise in the value of human time, and the large movements of people, for example, out of agriculture into other occupations.

Entrepreneurs have been around in economics for a long time, long enough to claim some theory as their own. Entrepreneurial theory in retrospect reveals that, on some important attributes of entrepreneurship, early economists had advantages over more recent over-specialized views. Insurable risk is not at issue. Uninsurable risk, however, is beset with analytical difficulties. The omission of Knight's[4] *True Uncertainty* is critical.

The lower bounds of the value of the time of entrepreneurs are established by the earnings they forgo while their time is devoted to entrepreneurship. There are serious flaws in identifying and treating the value of the productivity of entrepreneurs.

Our inquiry is strongly motivated by unsettled questions pertaining to disequilibria that are consequences of modern increases in income. What are the basic attributes of such disequilibria? When do such disequilibria become evident? These and related issues will be on our agenda. Can such disequilibria be prevented in ways that would not reduce the gains to be had from technological advances, from the proliferation of human capital, and from all forms of economic specialization? The answer will be that prevention would be too costly to be pursued as a policy objective.

Alternative types of economic organization loom large throughout this study. The incentives that induce entrepreneurs to reallocate their resources is a critical issue. A test entails the capacity and efficiency of such incentives in restoring equilibrium.

4   *Entrepreneurial Abilities*

Like intelligence, entrepreneurial ability is one of the general attributes of human beings. Observable behavior in response to changes in economic conditions indicates that most able-bodied adults do what is here deemed to be entrepreneurship. They break their routine and proceed to reallocate their own time and their other resources when they perceive that it is worthwhile to do so.

The innate and acquired abilities of people, be they individuals or families in charge of firms or households or self-employed, are important in restoring equilibrium. We now have competent studies that show measurable positive effects of experience, training, schooling, and of the state of health of people on their allocative abilities. The effects of schooling on the success of farmers in various parts of the world, as they take advantage of a new high-yielding crop variety, tell a consistent story. Thus, a consensus emerges that schooling increases the rate of adoption of high-yielding crop varieties by a rate that can be measured. There are few economic propositions that are as valid empirically as is the proposition that the entrepreneurial ability of farmers is enhanced by their schooling.

The economic domain of most human beings is small. When they perceive that they are no longer allocatively efficient, they act to bring their small domain into equilibrium. The motive of these small entrepreneurs is not that of restoring a general economic equilibrium. They are concerned about the disequilibria in their private domain.

It must be kept in mind that entrepreneurs are not accorded the status of an occupation. What entrepreneurs earn is not identified in national income accounting. Nor are their entrepreneurial earnings identified in micro empirical studies using standard production function techniques, which as a rule report a residual. What part of the reported residual may be entrepreneurial earnings is left undetermined. My primary concern is to understand the economic function of entrepreneurs in dealing with changes in economic conditions in a modernizing economy. I will not feature the coordination of the factors of production within the firm under a state of equilibrium as Coase has done.

5 As a Critique

A substantial part of this study may be viewed as a restrained critique of some aspects of economic thinking. There are concepts, assumptions, and analytics that are at issue.

The processes of economic modernization are immensely complex. Many of these processes continue to be beyond the analytical capacity of growth models.

The treatment of advances in technology is at issue. An all-inclusive analysis of all costs that advances in technology entail and of all increases in income derived from these advances provides proof that advances in technology are strictly endogenous.

Economic modernization reduces the economic importance of food-producing land, notably so in high income economies. The positive effects of this process on increases in income and on the distribution of personal income are among the neglected aspects of economics. Economic studies greatly underrate the importance of specialization that characterizes the modernization process.

Adam Smith could not have anticipated the vast specialization that has developed since he presented his famous theorem that the division of labor is limited by the extent of the market. Observable interactions between specialization and increases in income should have made economists aware that this theorem could explain in large measure the increases in specialization. Allyn Young[5] perceived this important latent implication. Five decades have elapsed since Young's highly significant paper appeared. Why have economists not pursued Young's analytics? Young may have anticipated the reason, to wit: "I suspect, indeed, that the apparatus which economists have built . . . may stand in the way of a clear view of the more general and elementary aspects of the phenomena. . . ."[6]

Increases in income, extensions of markets, and additional specialization interact. Each has a positive effect on the others. These effects are the basic sources of the self-sustaining properties of economic modernization.

Restoring equilibrium entails both macro and micro economics. It may also entail legal and other institutions, including public policy. The reason for concentrating on the micro part is that the implications of micro economics are usually stronger and more readily testable than those derived from macro economics. It is so empirically because of the greater divisibility of the entities inherent in micro economics. The analytics of human capital in restoring equilibrium, including the importance of property rights in human capital, receive major attention throughout this study.

People who are bound by the institution of slavery have no property rights in their human capital. Poor people, who account for most of the world's population, in general have some property rights. But their individual human capital component is very small. In high income countries where investments in human capital have been large, and where the rise in the value of human time has been pronounced, the property rights of people in their human capital are being enlarged.

In high income countries where wages, salaries, and earnings of the self-employed including entrepreneurs account for three-fourths and more of personal income, important institutional changes in favor of human capital property rights have occurred during recent decades. The political and legal origins of these changes are fairly evident. Self-interest should motivate scholars and scientists, including economists, to determine ways and means of extending intellectual property rights beyond existing patents and copyrights, beyond existing safety in the work place, beyond tenure rights, and beyond soft honors. Various unprotected intellectual property rights remain for which additional financial rewards are needed.

As the economic value of human time rises, we are in the realm of new and better opportunities. The range of private and social choice is enlarged. It is, indeed, an optimistic set of circumstances that all too few people of the world enjoy. But we are not free of institutional stresses and strains. Since we can specify and identify these institutional processes we can also analyze their results in terms of efficiency, income, and welfare.

Notes and References

1 I draw on parts of my paper "Human Capital in Restoring Equilibrium," SUNY, Buffalo Conference, May 26–27, 1989.

2 John Hicks, *Capital and Growth*, Oxford University Press, Oxford, 1965, Preface, v.

3 In micro production, technological advances are cost reducing.

4 Frank H. Knight, *Risk Uncertainty and Profit*, re-issue by the London School of Economics and Political Science, University of London, reprinted 1933, Preface, xiii.

5 Allyn Young, "Increasing Returns and Economic Progress," *Economic Journal*, December 1928, 527–42.

6 Ibid., p. 527.

2

What Restoring Equilibrium Entails

It would be pointless to burden our inquiry with disequilibria if none were known to exist. The fact that they occur is not proof that a general equilibrium theory is for that reason invalid as a logical entity. If our observable economy were in a state of general equilibrium, there would be no point in knowing the economics of restoring equilibrium.

When a disequilibrium occurs, it may be treated by means of special assumptions. The standard treatment is to rely on a *tendency assumption*, based on the proposition that there is such a tendency towards equilibrium throughout the economy. That such a tendency of sorts exists is not at issue. If it is a strong tendency, there is merit in using this assumption to simplify the analytical task. If it is not a strong tendency, however, the analyst is in trouble. This issue is considered further below.

As noted in the introduction, an alternative way is to transform any disequilibrium into a hypothetical equilibrium by means of various concepts of transaction costs, of information, and of subjective risks and expectations. Regardless of what is learned using this approach, it avoids the problem of restoring equilibrium.

Changes in economic conditions are the major source of disequilibria. The origins of such changes, following Schumpeter, are either from within or from outside the economy. Nature is a minor source. The actions of man account for nearly all of them, both for those that originate from within and for those that originate outside the economy.

Restoring an equilibrium entails both macro and micro economics, which may or may not include legal and other institutions, including governments and policy. The reason that this study concentrates on the micro economics part is that the theoretical implications of micro economics are much more readily testable than are those derived from macro economics. It is so because of the divisibility of the functional entities inherent in micro economics. What individuals and families do within firms, households, or as self-employed persons gives rise to many sets of data. For example, the effects of schooling on the success of farmers in various parts of the world, as they take advantage of a new high-yielding crop variety, are being analyzed. The relevant supply of usable agricultural data is large. Since I have specialized in the economics of farm people, most of my appeals to empirical results are based on farm and farm household economic behavior.

The dichotomy between micro and macro economics is not mutually exclusive; moreover, there are various types of micro disequilibria. Most of this study deals with types of micro disequilibria that occur as a consequence of economic modernization.[1]

At this micro level, the economic domain of the human agent is small. When this agent perceives that within his domain he is no longer allocatively efficient because of a change in conditions, he acts to bring his small domain into equilibrium. In this study what he does is treated as entrepreneurship. The motive of micro entrepreneurs is not that of restoring a general economic equilibrium. They are concerned about the disequilibria in their own private domain.

When it comes to the possibilities (opportunities) available to economic agents to restore equilibrium, much depends on the prevailing economic organization. There is strong evidence that choice of organization matters greatly.

Policy oriented economic inquiry understandably searches for ways of preventing disequilibria during the process of economic modernization. Aside from the organizational choice between a centrally controlled and a market oriented economy, are there ways that a market oriented economy could prevent all micro disequilibria? The results of this study indicate that it may not be possible to have economic modernization with no disequilibria. A centrally controlling economy can conceal such disequilibria but it too cannot keep them from occurring.

One is well advised to keep in mind that people throughout the world are economizing. What each person does in his own domain as he economizes is grist for the analytical mill of economists who specialize in micro economics. We should also be mindful that the analytics of micro economics have a substantial advantage over those of macro economics. The foundations of micro theory and the supporting evidence are usually stronger than those of macro economics. As a consequence, what is known about micro economic behavior is subject to fewer doubts compared with our knowledge about macro behavior.

1 Capacity, Ability, and Efficiency Issues

The capacity of an economy to restore equilibrium, as already noted, is in large measure a function of how the economy is organized. The observable difference on this score between a centrally controlled and a market oriented economy is large. A general consensus has emerged in economics that a market oriented economy has an advantage in its capacity and efficiency in coping with disequilibria. The innate and acquired abilities of human agents, be they individuals or families in charge of firms, or households, or those who are self-employed, are exceedingly important in restoring equilibrium. Human capital inquiry to ascertain the economic value of work experience, schooling, more education, and health has added substantially to our knowledge of the economic value of these human capital components.

Despite what has been learned, the core of economics is virtually silent on these capacity, ability, and efficiency issues in restoring equilibrium. The main reason why the economics of restoring equilibrium has not been considered is a consequence, as noted above, of the over-reliance on the assumption that a tendency to equilibrium exists.

This tendency assumption is pervasive throughout economics. In Knight's[2] view, "There can be no question of a real tendency toward equilibrium in detailed relationships, or even apparently in the system as a whole." The dependence on this assumption is neatly stated by Boulding:[3] "The compass in all our travels has been the concept of equilibrium. . . . The 'equilibrium' position of any price, wage, firm, industry, or system is the position toward which it is tending."

That there exists a tendency towards equilibrium is not at issue. The problems with which we began, however, are not resolved by an appeal to this "tendency." Hicks's[4] argument is telling. "Something has to be specified about reactions to disequilibrium before the existence of a tendency to equilibrium can be asserted. . . . Even if the equilibrium exists, and the tendency to equilibrium exists, we may still have insufficient ground to justify the equilibrium assumption if the convergence to equilibrium is very slow."

The economics of restoring equilibrium is a much neglected part of economic analysis.

My inquiry presented in "The Value of the Ability to Deal with Disequilibria"[5] concentrated on the equilibrating functions of economic agents. It was a first step. "Investment in Entrepreneurial Ability"[6] followed. The arguments presented in these two studies remain valid, although all too little analysis was presented of the effects of the organization of an economy on its capacity and efficiency in restoring equilibrium.

The theoretical importance of disequilibrium analysis is beginning to receive considerable attention. The state of this development is clearly evident in Franklin Fisher's[7] recent monograph. His first step in laying the foundation for his approach to economic disequilibria is an adequate theory of stability. Stability theory requires "... that the equilibria of economic models are not only stable but that convergence to a neighborhood of equilibrium is achieved relatively quickly...." The speed of convergence is a critical issue. Fisher's[8] analysis of the development of the stability literature is especially useful in showing the gaps that separate theory and evidence.

Notes and References

1 The phrase "economic growth" is basically a biological metaphor that burdens economic analysis with biological connotations. As we proceed, we shall opt for *increases in income* that are derived from endogenous economic events.

2 Frank H. Knight, *Risk, Uncertainty and Profit*, re-issue by the London School of Economics and Political Science, University of London, reprinted 1933, Preface, xxiii.

3 Kenneth E. Boulding, *Economic Analysis*, revised edition, Harper and Brothers, New York, 1948, ch. 30, p. 637.

4 John Hicks, *Capital and Growth*, Oxford University Press, Oxford, 1965, ch. II, pp. 18–19.

5 Theodore W. Schultz, "The Value of the Ability to Deal with Disequilibria," *Journal of Economic Literature*, 13 (3), September 1975, 827–46.

6 Theodore W. Schultz, "Investment in Entrepreneurial Ability," *Scandinavian Journal of Economics*, 82, 1980, 437–48.

7 Franklin M. Fisher, *Disequilibrium Foundations of Equilibria Economics*, Econometric Society Monographs No. 6, Cambridge University Press, Cambridge, 1989.

8 Ibid., ch. 1, p. 4.

3

Dealing with Economic Disequilibria

In recent "growth" economics, the nature, significance, and source of disequilibria receive little attention. What is being done instead is to develop models under the assumption that the process of economic modernization has the attributes of a steady, balanced, and continuous equilibrium process. Disequilibria are left to struggle beyond the pale of such models.

A retrospective view of economic modernization reveals that, time and again, it is at the mercy of wars and their aftermath. There are reoccurring economic shocks from serious depressions and from unexpected, unfavorable, and favorable events. Economic changes in production and consumption often occur abruptly. Not least are the awesome economic distortions and disequilibria that occur in centrally controlled economies.

At different times and places in the history of the world, economic modernization that increases income has not been and is not now a homogeneous process. Time, place, and opportunities matter. By economic modernization we mean that major sources of increases in income are derived from increases in specialization – a specialization made possible by advances in knowledge that enhance the quality and productivity of physical and human capital components. Physical capital is improved by increasing the effective supply of various natural resources, including land, by man-made substitutes. Human capital is increased by the provision of specialized sectors devoted to organized research and education.

When it comes to empirical analyses, most of the appeals to evidence in this study are based on economic experiences since the Second World War. Our observations tell us that economic conditions changed yesterday, they are changing today, and there is high probability that they will change tomorrow, and that the resulting disequilibria are of many different types.

One must also keep in mind that the motivation of private entrepreneurs is not economic growth. Their motives are not to improve the performance of the economy, or to increase national employment and the level of wages, or to prevent inflation and deflation. Self-interest of entrepreneurs holds the key to their motivations. It is the profitability and satisfactions that they expect to derive from their entrepreneurial endeavor that motivate them.

Schumpeter,[1] in his theory of economic development, attributed primary importance to the innovations of entrepreneurs. But at best their innovations are only one of the determinants that characterize the complex process of economic modernization. It is evident that investment in human capital contributes substantially to the observable productivity of an economy as a consequence of the increase in the quality of human time that is devoted to economic activities.[2] Only a small fraction of the investments in human capital is made by Schumpeter's entrepreneurs. Furthermore, advances in the sciences and in related useful knowledge have become a major source of improvements in technology that reduce real costs and which in turn enhance real income over time. To restrict entrepreneurs to being only innovators omits various other contributions they make as they deal with economic disequilibria.

Standard theory does not specify the sources of economic disequilibria, including when and where they will occur, what their magnitude will be, whether they will occur gradually or abruptly and whether they will have a short or long existence. The resolution of these issues awaits theory and empirical inquiry. Like the income elasticity of the demand for consumer goods and services, what we know that is useful is based primarily on empirical evidence.

The assumption that economic disequilibria are homogeneous will not do when it comes to analyzing the behavior of economic agents as they deal with economic disequilibria. It is nevertheless tempting to assume homogeneity to simplify the analytical task. But it is an error prone procedure, akin to the homogeneity assumption in capital theory which Hicks[3] labelled a "disaster." "Like other metaphysical entities, it is a boat that is loose from its moorings.... If there is just one homogeneous 'capital' ... there can be no problems of malinvestment."

The assumption of homogeneity is also beset with errors when it comes to determining the economic value of labor and land. Counting acres, or the number of workers in the labor force, or aggregating various capital goods into "one capital good" in determining the productivity of these factors is error prone research. Nor are economic disequilibria homogeneous. They differ with respect to (a) their origins, (b) the extent to which the transitory income components inherent in the disequilibria can be transformed into permanent income components, and (c) the rate at which equilibration is optimal. But heterogeneity opens a Pandora's box.

1   Vicissitudes of Nature

In a modern economy, relatively few economic disequilibria originate out of the vicissitudes of Nature. The agricultural sector is in some ways an exception. This sector, however, is relatively small in most advanced modern economies. Although this study features some of the agricultural-specific disequilibria that are caused by Nature, they play a declining role as the agricultural sector becomes a small part of the economy.

The periodicity of the seasons is well known. So are the probabilities of floods, storms, hail, and cyclones, and fires caused by Nature. Crop-killing frosts and severe droughts do occur.

The probability and magnitude of another subset, for example a series of bad or of good crops occurring at the same time throughout much of the world, are only partially known. Changes in the location and movements of ocean fish caused by changes in water temperature are also partially known. In general these changes are not insurable risks.

There are also events caused by Nature which are beyond the reasoned expectations of economic agents. This subset includes the place and time of specific occurrence of destructive earthquakes, of devastating eruptions of a particular volcano, and of unprecedented winter snowfalls in mountains followed by destructive sudden spring melting of the snow.

Some biological events also belong in this subset, namely, the occurrence of a sudden deadly epidemic that kills vast numbers of people or one that destroys livestock. Nature is also host to sudden crop blights, the Mediterranean fruit fly, and other pests and insects.

There is a large body of evidence pertaining to the actions of farmers, as they endeavor to cope with the vicissitudes of Nature. Implications of such evidence are considered in later chapters.

Most economic disequilibria are consequences of social, political, and economic actions of human beings. Changes that occur as consequences of these various actions can be approached using Schumpeter's dichotomy of changes that occur from within or from without the economy. We shall presently elaborate further on the attributes of different types of man-made disequilibria and their economic implications.

Small private entrepreneurs play a large role in restoring equilibrium. We need to know more about their ability and efficiency in performing this role. We turn to some preliminary entrepreneurial issues.

2   *Elusiveness of Entrepreneurs*

There are many different economic entities, the specifications of which are established and for which there are useful statistics. The work activities of populations are available by occupations. But whatever it is that entrepreneurs do, their activities do not appear as an occupation. Managers are listed, but where management leaves off and entrepreneurship begins and prevails is not reckoned.

As things stand, entrepreneurship is not an occupation. During the period that a person is an entrepreneur, he is rarely only an entrepreneur. His entrepreneurial action has as a rule a short time dimension. The income he derives from his entrepreneurship is transitory. Economists are not privy to his subjective expectations. His entrepreneurial ability is enhanced by experience, schooling, and the robustness of his health. An all-inclusive specification of the abilities of entrepreneurs would encompass all innate and acquired abilities of human beings that, for the purpose at hand, have a value in dealing with economic disequilibria.[4]

Systematic observations of the responses of entrepreneurs to changes in economic conditions that can be quantified and measured are hard to come by. Plausible impressions may be useful up to a point, but they are not a substitute for reliable measurements. Economic logic is required. But, as already noted, in evaluating the performance of entrepreneurs, judgments are distorted by ideologies which are either pro competitive market or pro centrally controlled economy. The number of private entrepreneurs in a market economy is large relative to the number of officials who are in charge of a centrally controlled economy. Some judgments overrate the economic importance of the occasional "captains of industry" and of the anonymous administrators of a centrally planned and managed economy.

In terms of both observations and economic logic, private entrepreneurs are not a unique breed of purposive people. The difference between them and other people who engage in economic activities depends in substantial part on the difference in economic circumstances. Whereas nonhuman factors of production and of consumer goods are passive entities, human actions are purposive. When people engage in routine work and when their consumption, savings, and investment are also routine, the things that they do are nevertheless purposive human acts. Their acts are deemed by them to be "optimum" under the economic options available to them. When their perceived options change, they may become entrepreneurs.

Entrepreneurial acts are practical and in that sense they are mundane economic acts. In their economic domain entrepreneurs are not artists, or scientists, or specialized intellectuals. Creativity is not the hallmark of entrepreneurs. It is misleading to glamorize entrepreneurs as a creative breed who are endowed with originality, create new ideas, and are *the prime innovators* in economic affairs. To assert without evidence that entrepreneurs are more alert and endowed with better vision about future economic possibilities, and that they generate more luck for themselves than other human agents who are not entrepreneurs, is to romanticize entrepreneurship. It is the better part of economic thinking to treat entrepreneurs as practical human agents who are motivated by economic incentives, and thus whose acts are grist for economic analysis. To glamorize them with creativity and other noble talents may be appealing, but it complicates economic analysis with unnecessary ambiguities.

In an endeavor to understand the economic behavior of entrepreneurs, there are no reasons for treating their preferences differently from the way that economists treat the preferences of other human beings – be they workers, savers, investors, or consumers. Economists are not renowned for their psychological knowledge pertaining to preferences. For economists, preferences are revealed by what people actually do as economic agents. Thus, since entrepreneurs are economic agents, their preferences must be observed for purposes of economic analyses. On this point, namely on observed and measured entrepreneurial behavior, the state of economics is weak. It is a case where theory and facts all too rarely talk to each other.

The frequently repeated implication of true uncertainty is that the consequent windfalls and losses, for an economy in its entirety, cancel each other out. But there is no evidence that supports or falsifies this implication. Moreover, it is doubtful that there ever could be observable facts to test its validity.

J. B. Clark's[5] concept of the entrepreneur as being empty-handed with no capital of his own is falsified by the observation that *every entrepreneur possesses a stock of human capital*. Like the Ricardian concept of the unchanging original properties of the soil, Clark's entrepreneur does not exist. The economic literature that indentures the entrepreneur to true uncertainty greatly restricts economic thinking about what it is that entrepreneurs actually do.

3   Why do People become Entrepreneurs?

The question of who become entrepreneurs does not arise in general equilibrium theory because the entrepreneur is theoretically superfluous. In reality, however, there are all manner of entrepreneurs. Accordingly, this question is indeed relevant.

In their concern about practical economic affairs, the early economists took entrepreneurs as they observed them. They observed entrepreneurs as active economic agents who organized enterprises and who were responsible for their performance. For these early economists, there were no compelling reasons to develop sophisticated concepts of the existence of pure entrepreneurs. Correspondingly, they were not concerned about the proof of the existence of equilibrium under competition.

One of the arguments on why particular people become entrepreneurs is the propensity to gamble. In a treatise on *The Human Gamble*, Reuven Brenner[6] argues that people have a propensity to gamble when their income position is reduced. According to Brenner, this propensity to gamble explains what people do when they experience a decline in their relative position in the distribution of wealth. This human trait under these conditions ". . . leads us to gamble on *novel ideas* in business, science, arts, and the organization of social institutions." The critical issue in this argument is the effect of an adverse change in the distribution of wealth on what people do in response to such a change. Following Irving Fisher,[7] wealth is defined as a stock of capital and the services derived from capital as flows (streams) of income. Thus, Brenner's argument can be formulated as an income effect, namely, the propensity to gamble is revealed when an individual or a group of people experience a decline in their relative position in the personal distribution of income.

Brenner presents evidence in support of his explanation, including the income effects of discrimination against particular ethnic groups. When they are legally barred from land ownership, from positions in government, and from other high paying occupations, they turn to finance, trade, and other business activities. His analysis of anti-semitism rests on the argument that the resulting inequality in income reveals the propensity to gamble. A considerable body of other evidence is also featured in his treatise.

Brenner's income inequality, however, is only a part of the story of why people become entrepreneurs. It excludes the many circumstances when changes in economic conditions provide new opportunities making it possible and worthwhile for particular people to enhance their income position. It is well documented that people become entrepreneurs under such circumstances.[8]

Some of the captains of large corporations are undoubtedly innovators, but, in making them the prime innovators, Schumpeter overlooked the economic importance of the innovations of small corporations, small private firms, and of many self-employed people. At present, for example, there are large numbers of small computer manufacturing firms, many of them producing small parts for computers, with successful records as innovators. With no appeal to evidence, it is all too easy to glamorize the economic importance of the captains of large corporations on this issue.

To think of entrepreneurship as a pure arbitrage activity excludes most entrepreneurial acts. Few people become entrepreneurs to engage in pure arbitrage.

The uncertainty residual that occurs as a consequence of unforeseeable changes in future economic conditions cannot account for the actual contributions that entrepreneurs make. People do not and cannot become entrepreneurs to gain or lose from true uncertainty which is unknowable.

No matter what part of a modernizing economy is being investigated, we observe that economic conditions change, that each change entails a specific disequilibrium, and that human agents act to regain equilibrium in their domain. What they do is in essence entrepreneurship. Economic analyses of what they do as entrepreneurs calls for additional elements of theory and evidence.

Notes and References

1   Joseph A. Schumpeter, *The Theory of Economic Development*, Harvard University Press, Cambridge, MA, 1967.
2   On this issue my "The Economics of the Value of Human Time," chapter 4 in *Investing in People*, University of California Press, Berkeley, CA, 1980, is in large part an analysis of the fivefold increase in real earnings per hour of work in the United States since 1900.

3   John Hicks, *Capital and Growth*, Oxford University Press, Oxford, 1965, 34–5.

4   When a scientist decides to devote his time and complementary resources to pursuing a particular hypothesis from among various alternative hypotheses, he is in essence a research entrepreneur. We shall deal with this aspect of research later.

5   J. B. Clark, "Insurance and Profits," *Quarterly Journal of Economics*, vii, 1893.

6   Reuven Brenner, *History – The Human Gamble*, The University of Chicago Press, Chicago, IL, 1984.

7   Irving Fisher, *The Nature of Capital and Income*, Macmillan, New York and London, 1906.

8   Evidence on this point will be presented later in this study.

4

Economic Value of an Entrepreneur's Time

What an entrepreneur does when he engages in an entrepreneurial activity takes time. The economic value of that component of time is here at issue. For analysis, we turn to Gary Becker's[1] theory of the allocation of time. It is applicable to the time that a person devotes to a utility-producing activity. It is applicable to work for wages, salaries, and to self-employment, and also to the time devoted to household work. It is applicable to the time spent in acquiring an education including on-the-job training. So, too, to consumption for it also takes time. But the theory has been used sparingly in getting at the value of the time that people devote to entrepreneurial activities.

Alternative work opportunities imply that the earnings the entrepreneur could have had from such work are earnings forgone. As such, they are a measure of the opportunity cost of the entrepreneur's time.

Work which is done in an established regular manner may be viewed as being repetitive and routine. Where specialization entails specialized skills, the work of those who have acquired such skills may also become repetitive and routine. But what an entrepreneur does is not repetitive, nor does it become routine.

There are many unsettled questions pertaining to entrepreneurship. What exactly is it that entrepreneurs do? Is it an identifiable economic activity? Are entrepreneurs productive economic agents or are they collecting unearned rent? Does the market reveal the economic value of whatever it is that entrepreneurs do?

1   Schumpeter Versus Hicks

Schumpeter's[2] approach to economic development exemplifies the economic importance of entrepreneurs as innovators. He extended his approach in "Economic Theory and Entrepreneurial History."[3] But when he came to his description of vanishing investment opportunities, with its "Crumbling Walls," there was "... nothing left for the entrepreneur to do."[4] Here, Schumpeter surrenders all too readily to his vision of vanishing investment opportunities. We shall take advantage, however, of a good deal of his early thinking on economic development in determining the demand for and supply of entrepreneurial ability.

Schumpeter emphasized the favorable changes in economic conditions that entrepreneurs create as innovators. Most economists, however, have not opted for Schumpeter's approach. *Value and Capital* (1939), *Capital and Growth* (1965), *Capital and Time* (1973), a trilogy by Hicks,[5] exemplifies economics without entrepreneurs. There are various methods for analyzing dynamic economics based on continuous, steady, growth equilibrium.

From Arrow and Debreu,[6] we have proof that a general competitive equilibrium exists in theory. Within the core of the theory, there are no disequilibria. It is a rigorous conception of a general economic equilibrium which is in no way dependent on entrepreneurs. If such an economy exists, it would not be a modernizing economy, which entails extensions of markets, specialization, and income-increasing events that arise from new forms of physical and human capital. In view of the limitations of economic growth models a search for evidence using such models is beset with difficulties.

2   Room for Doubts

Inferences from empirical evidence are not free of doubts. An epistemology of the nature and grounds of economic knowledge is essential to comprehend and understand human actions in economic affairs. It entails perceptions based on observations, reasons based on logic, and judgments based on values. For entrepreneurship this means that for want of observable evidence perceptions are intuitive, for want of economic logic there can be no economic reasons for what entrepreneurs do, and for want of a received set of values there can be no accepted judgments of their performance. The economic analysis of entrepreneurship is weak for lack of observations. A useful general theory of entrepreneurship is wanting. Ideological controversies distort the values required to evaluate the contributions that entrepreneurs make.

Specialization in economics has enhanced the productivity of economists. Appeals to data and quantitative analysis have flourished as dependence on introspection and intuition has declined. Some properties of theory are beyond the reach of evidence. Moreover, there are difficult unsolved problems that pertain to economic decisions and actions of people as economic conditions change over time.

3   Language Ambiguities

Notwithstanding the advances in economics, there are alternative modes of economic thinking that are more comrehensive than economic growth models. For our purpose, however, the language of economics about entrepreneurs is beset with ambiguities that limit its usefulness in dealing with observable behavior. When theory banishes the entrepreneur, he finds refuge elsewhere in economics. A few economists assign a lively useful role to entrepreneurs, namely, as innovators who increase the productivity of the economy. But do entrepreneurs create disequilibria, or do they perceive the existence and the profitable opportunities that disequilibria entail? Is there evidence that entrepreneurs who innovate have a unique ability to perceive the existence of such opportunities? Kirzner[7] argues that they have this unique ability, but he provides no evidence. Others argue that people who gamble on probabilities are entrepreneurs. Families with a relatively large transitory income component are deemed to be entrepreneurial families. Ambiguities abound in what is meant by "uninsurable risk," by the "probabilities" of the subjective expectations of entrepreneurs, by "true uncertainty," and by entrepreneurial "profit." Despite the classic work of Frank Knight,[8] the meanings of uninsurable risk, true uncertainty, and unexpected profits and losses continue to be enshrined in ambiguities.

We shall concentrate on a large class of entrepreneurs, namely those who restore equilibrium in their own microeconomic domain.[9] Our argument is that such disequilibria create demands for what entrepreneurs do. What they do is to take equilibrating actions when they perceive that it would be profitable for them to do so. If no disequilibria of this type were to occur, there would be no demand for entrepreneurs of this class. Our search is to identify and to gauge the economic value of the ability of people in restoring equilibrium as disequilibria occur during the process of economic modernization.

The value of the time that entrepreneurs devote to economic modernization is substantial and important. The rewards that they derive for their contributions are the driving force in reallocating resources as modernization is achieved. *An entrepreneur's expected earnings for the time he devotes to entrepreneurial endeavors is here deemed to be not less than the value of the alternative earnings from his human capital that he forgoes.*

Notes and References

1 Gary S. Becker, "A Theory of the Allocation of Time," *Economic Journal*, 75, September 1965, 493–517.
2 Joseph A. Schumpeter, *The Theory of Economic Development*, Harvard University Press, Cambridge, MA, 1967.
3 Joseph A. Schumpeter, in *Explorations in Enterprises*, edited by Hugh G. J. Aitken, Harvard University Press, Cambridge, MA, 1967, pp. 45–64.
4 Joseph A. Schumpeter, *Capitalism, Socialism, and Democracy*, Harper and Brothers, New York, 1942, ch. XII, 131–42.
5 In *Value and Capital*, 1939, pp. 194–201, Hicks does mention "... the entrepreneur maximizing his surplus of receipts over costs. ..."
6 Kenneth J. Arrow and Gerard Debreu, "Existence of an Equilibrium for a Competitive Economy," *Econometrica*, 22 (3), 1954, 265–90.
7 Israel M. Kirzner, *Perception, Opportunity, and Profit*, University of Chicago Press, Chicago, IL, 1974.
8 Frank H. Knight, *Risk, Uncertainty and Profits*, Houghton Mifflin, Boston and New York, 1921.
9 Theodore W. Schultz, "The Value of the Ability to Deal with Disequilibria," *Journal of Economic Literature*, 13, September 1975, 927–46.

5

Entrepreneurial Theory in Retrospect

Neither the idea of a stationary state nor that of a steady growth economy is dependent on entrepreneurs. In dealing with economic conditions that may give rise to an unstable economy, there is no scarcity of ideas pertaining to institutions and to economic organizations that are required to achieve an orderly economy. Entrepreneurs perform a fundamental role in restoring equilibrium, as income is being increased.

Entrepreneurial ability as a form of human capital is a new idea. The linkage between entrepreneurship and true uncertainty windfalls and losses continues to be beset with ambiguities. Theory has not provided a rigorous and testable distinction between management and entrepreneurship. All too often the personal attributes of the entrepreneur are not reckoned with, nor is the value of his time, starting with the opportunities forgone when he devotes his time to entrepreneurial endeavors. Also missing is an explicit formulation of the economic conditions that determine the economic value of the contributions that entrepreneurs, large and small, make to observable economic activities.

The treatment of entrepreneurs by the early economists may be judged either in terms of what was then the state of economic thought and the then prevailing organization of the economy, or by the present state of economic theory and the complexities of present economic organization. To impose the latter judgment on the first category seems presumptuous. Neither marginal utility theory[1] nor marginal productivity theory were a part of the early economists' analytical tools. As already noted, most of them were concerned about practical economic affairs. They observed that people in charge of production owned much of the capital they used; as economic agents they worked and they decided how best to allocate the resources at their disposal. For the early economists to have viewed those in charge of enterprises as having no capital and as doing no work was inconsistent with what they observed. Their view of entrepreneurship has more merit than that of economists since then who have postulated the *entrepreneur* as having no capital and as doing no work.

An important survey of the thinking of early economists by Bert Hoselitz[2] gives us the French concepts of the entrepreneur before Cantillon, the English concepts before Adam Smith, the theory of entrepreneurship of the Physiocrats, and the links between it and the theories of Cantillon and Say. The entrepreneur presented in these various concepts is a description of what the early economists thought they observed. A doctoral dissertation by Susan Cole[3] not only covers the early history drawing on Hoselitz, but also features the entrepreneurial ideas of Hawley, Knight, Schumpeter, and Mises and concludes with an extended critique and synthesis. Cole is awed by the "pure" entrepreneur – which appears to lead her not to see the human capital that entrepreneurs possess and the economic value of their time. Robert F. Herbert and Albert N. Link's[4] treatment of *The Entrepreneur* is a comprehensive and critical assessment of entrepreneurial theories.

1   Still an Elusive Concept

But to determine the value of what entrepreneurs do continues to be difficult. The dialogue between theory and observable entrepreneurial behavior is not one of the more cogent and useful parts of economics. The supply of this ability is rarely considered; nor is the demand for it an integral part of economic theory. William Baumol[5] puts it neatly: "The references are scanty and more often they are totally absent. The theoretical firm is entrepreneurless ... the Prince of Denmark has been expunged from the discussion of *Hamlet*." There are, of course, well-defined problems that equilibrium theory deals with which require no entrepreneur for their solution. If there were competition and if the economy had arrived at an equilibrium, and if there were no changes that would disturb that equilibrium, entrepreneurial ability would have no economic value.

Thus, in large measure, economic theory either omits the entrepreneur or burdens him with esoteric niceties, the implications of which are rarely observable. The entrepreneur, as noted, is not required in equilibrium theory in order to solve the problems for which that theory is appropriate. In nearly all of the production function literature, the entrepreneur does not appear as an explicit economic agent. In the part of theory that deals with "pure profits," the entrepreneur is indentured to true uncertainty.

It is not sufficient to attribute some innovations to them, or to treat entrepreneurs as doing no more than collecting profits and bearing losses that occur as a consequence of true uncertainty. Although it is obvious that a part of the economic behavior of many people is neither repetitive nor routine, what is not obvious is that in addition to businessmen there are many other people who at different junctures during their life cycle are entrepreneurs. It is not obvious that the demand for what they do depends on the changes that characterize the particular economy, that the supply of entrepreneurial services depends on the number and ability of these economic agents, and that the economic value of their services is substantial.

The contribution of entrepreneurs in a changing economy is of major importance, although it is concealed in national income accounting. The rich array of studies by Simon

Kuznets[6] in his *Modern Economic Growth* is a notable exception. Basic parts of Kuznets's studies present estimates of the shares in national income contributed by entrepreneurs, including the self-employed, over long periods. His estimates include six high income countries. The indicated relevant shares are highest in France and Germany. They are also important in Switzerland, Canada, the United States, and the United Kingdom.

The economics of the acquisition of entrepreneurial ability is still in its infancy. There are returns to this form of human capital; the emergence of firms may also be partially explained in terms of organizational human capital.[7]

What entrepreneurs do must have some economic value in order for there to be earnings that accrue to the "scarce" entrepreneurial ability. In Erik Dahmen's[8] view, Schumpeter succeeded in showing that, as innovators, business enterprises produced the new and better technology. What Schumpeter could not have anticipated is the growth of research supported by the public sector. In the United States in 1983, for example, 69 percent of all basic research was funded by the federal government.[9] A large part of agricultural research throughout the world is being done by governments.[10]

2   Knightian True Uncertainty

Knightian uncertainty bedevils many economists in ascertaining the economic value of entrepreneurship. Knight's[11] modest preface in *Risk, Uncertainty, and Profit* states simply that, "The particular technical contribution to the theory of free enterprise which this essay purports to make is a fuller and more careful examination of the role of the *entrepreneur* or enterpriser, the recognized 'central figure' of the system and of the forces which fix the remuneration of his special function." Although much of Knight's[12] treatise is devoted to the function of entrepreneurs in a dynamic market economy, this part has received little attention. It is noteworthy that economists who draw on Knight rarely consider Knight's treatment of the role that entrepreneurs play in a dynamic economy, nor are they aware, so it would appear, of Knight's[13] remarkable 23 page preface to the London School of Economics 1933 re-issue of his treatise.

Knight analyzes the contributions of entrepreneurs in a dynamic market economy. He deals at length with the risk and the uncertainty problems inherent in nature, that is, natural resources, in technological changes, and in the instability of prices. He sees factor prices as more amenable to contracts than output prices. Thus, the interval of time between production based on contracted factors and the sale of the output is a special source of risk. He also sees advances in knowledge as the most pervasive and important part of the problem. The treatise is rich with insights on the limitations of information and of expectations, as change and progress occur under actual market conditions. He is, indeed, much concerned with the contributions of entrepreneurs to the equilibrating process, despite all manner of risk and of *true uncertainty*.

Knight devotes a long chapter (chapter V) to the theory of change and progress with uncertainty absent. In chapter XI he returns to this *"unchanging property of changing,"* noting that it would require a completely knowable world which is, in his view, a pure artifact of our minds, a refuge to which we flee from an unknowable world. Knight's *true uncertainty* is not a form of risk. His true uncertainty is unknowable and unmeasurable, and its result in choice cannot be treated as if it were a gamble on a knowable mathematical distribution. *Untrue* uncertainty is a misnomer; it is always a form of risk. All forms of risk are treated as having a probability distribution. An unsettled issue arises, however, in the distinction between risks the probability distribution of which is knowable to economists, and risks that economists cannot observe to determine their numerical probabilities. Milton Friedman[14] contends that this is not a valid distinction. He follows L. J. Savage in his view of personal probability, which denies any valid distinction along these lines. But to argue that this distinction is not valid for the decision of the entrepreneur does not solve the problem of the observer, that is, the economist, because he is not privy to what the entrepreneur *thinks* is probable.

Ludwig von Mises[15] attributes a pervasive role to entrepreneurs. The title of his treatise on economic principles, *Human Action*, is a clear indication that the actions of human agents are basic. The actions of entrepreneurs are deemed to be critical in a changing modern economy. Mises is explicit on the point that the entrepreneur does not exist in an "evenly rotating economy" (an economy in equilibrium), and that he cannot be eliminated from a market economy.

Mises's argument is that, in an economy in which changes are occurring, the factors of production "cannot come together spontaneously. They need to be combined by the purposive efforts of men aiming at certain ends and motivated by the urge to improve their state of satisfaction. In eliminating the entrepreneur one eliminates the driving force of the whole market system."[16] Mises's conception of the entrepreneur does not exclude human agents who are responsible for making decisions in small firms. Nor are Schumpeter's innovators in large corporations excluded. Nor are others who make such decisions.

3 Where Kirzner went Wrong

We turn now to the contribution of Israel Kirzner.[17] Kirzner states that his ideas of what entrepreneurs do are based in large part on those of Mises. His analysis of the function of entrepreneurs in a changing economy beset with disequilibria is cogent and useful. The merits of his study are twofold. It begins with a clear extensive presentation of economic theory based on equilibrium assumptions to show how that theory does not require entrepreneurs as active economic agents.

This is followed by the core of a "dynamic" theory dealing with various types of disequilibria, which are analyzed in the context of markets and prices in which entrepreneurs perform an essential economic function.

The observable facts of the economic process in a modern economy, as changes occur over time, strongly support the occurrence of the types of disequilibria that are featured by Kirzner. Nevertheless, his analysis fails with respect to the economic value of what entrepreneurs do, for he concludes, ". . . that at market level . . . entrepreneurship is not to be treated as a resource. . . . The market never recognizes entrepreneurial ability in the sense of an available useful resource."[18]

What went wrong in arriving at this conclusion? The economic value of the costs of opportunity time that entrepreneurs devote to being entrepreneurs is lost sight of. It is as if they devoted their time to being entrepreneurs with no expectation that they would receive any rewards for their endeavors. Kirzner is patently wrong in his view that there are no expected entrepreneurial rewards that accrue to entrepreneurs as economic agents.

It is necessary to distinguish between the unknowable residual arising from true uncertainty and the "rent or quasi-rent" that accrues to entrepreneurs as a reward for their entrepreneurial endeavors. In the economics of the firm, Friedman[19] distinguishes between actual noncontractual costs and expected contractual costs, and he treats the expected contractual costs "as a *rent* or *quasi-rent*" which is the motivating force behind the firm's decision.

The opportunity cost of entrepreneurial ability is noted by Becker.[20] The interactions of the supply of this class of ability and the demand for it determine the value of the time of entrepreneurs. Thus, entrepreneurial ability is a part of the stock of human capital.

For theory to be useful in accounting for the marginal productivity of entrepreneurs, the theory must distinguish between the true uncertainty residual and the contributions of entrepreneurs to productivity. These contributions are amenable to productivity analysis; what entrepreneurs earn depends on the value of their contribution to production.

An economy with no risk and no true uncertainty does not exist. These elements are ever present components in a changing economy. Appeals to *true* uncertainty in the literature of economics do not reckon its actual importance in economic affairs. The importance that is placed on the true uncertainty residual has not been accompanied by measurements. The presumed "large" true uncertainty residual may account for the neglect by economists of the economic value of time of entrepreneurs for which they earn a "rent," and for the neglect of the demand for and supply of entrepreneurial ability.

Furthermore, any true uncertainty residual is beyond the domain of standard marginal productivity analysis. This residual is not a reward for what entrepreneurs do. What they earn is a return for their contributions to production and to consumption activities.

On this issue Mark Blaug[21] is cogent and succinct. Unexpected profit is "... neither an opportunity cost, nor a real cost, ... it is a residual leftover after all contractual costs have been met...."

In thinking about what entrepreneurs do, it is imperative to hold fast to the basic reality that disequilibria are inevitable in a modern, ever changing economy. Such an economy is decidedly dependent on entrepreneurs who reallocate their resources. A theory to explain the actions of entrepreneurs must distinguish between their responses to insurable risk and their responses to uninsurable risk. The distinction between the effects of these two classes of risks and those of true uncertainty is also essential since there can be no response to the latter at the time entrepreneurs act; a key analytical problem is the nature of the uninsurable risks and their economic effects.

What entrepreneurs do has an economic value. This value accrues to them as a "reward" for their time and ability, that is, a reward for what they achieve. This reward is *earned*. Although this reward for the entrepreneurship of most human agents is small in the aggregate in a modernizing economy, it accounts for an important part of the increases in national income. The omission of this part of the increases in national income implies that entrepreneurs have not received their due in economic analyses.

Notes and References

1   George J. Stigler, *The Economist as Preacher*, chapter 7, "The Adoption of Marginal Utility Theory," University of Chicago Press, Chicago, IL, 1982, pp. 72–85.

2   Bert F. Hoselitz, "The Early History of Entrepreneurial Theory," *Exploration*, 3, April 1951, 193–220.

3   Susan G. Cole, "The History, Development and Significance of Entrepreneurial Theory," Ph.D. Dissertation, Harvard University, March 1977.

4   Robert F. Herbert and Albert N. Link, *The Entrepreneur*, 2nd edn, Praeger, New York, 1988.

5   William J. Baumol's brief paper, "Entrepreneurship and Economic Theory," *American Economic Review, Papers and Proceedings*, 68, May 1968, 68–71, is perceptive in seeing that the entrepreneurial function is an essential part of the process of economic modernization.

6   Simon Kuznets, *Modern Economic Growth, Rate, Structure, and Spread*, Yale University Press, New Haven, CT, 1966.

7   Edward C. Prescott and Michael Vincher, "Organizational Capital," *Journal of Political Economy*, 88, June 1980, 446–61.

8   Erik Dahmen, *Entrepreneurial Activity and the Development of Swedish Industry, 1919–1939*, translated into English by Axel Leijonhufvud, published for the American Economic Association by Irwin, Holmwood, IL, 1970.

9   Theodore W. Schultz, "The Productivity of Research: The

Politics and Economics of Research," *Minerva*, 18, Winter 1980, 644–51.

10 Theodore W. Schultz, "The Economics of Research and Agricultural Productivity," *International Agricultural Development Service*, Occasional Paper, New York, 1979.

11 Frank H. Knight, *Risk, Uncertainty and Profit*, Houghton Mifflin, Boston and New York, 1921, ix and 381 pages.

12 Knight uses the word "dynamic"; so did Schumpeter in the 1911 German edition. In the English edition, Schumpeter goes to considerable length to explain why the word "dynamic" was misleading and he opts for "changes" in the economy.

13 Frank H. Knight, *Risk, Uncertainty and Profit*, London School of Economics and Political Science, Reprint 16, 1933. Knight's reasoned pessimism about the limitations of economics and intellectual inquiry in general, written a half a century ago, is decidedly applicable at the present time. Parts of page xxiii bear directly on the issues here under consideration. "There can be no question of a real tendency toward equilibrium in detailed relationships, or even apparently in the system as a whole.... The forces and resistance relations in the movement toward equilibrium are ... mental, affecting the learning process (elimination of 'errors') in the minds of consumers, managers and owners of productive resources."

14 Milton Friedman, *Price Theory*, Aldine, Chicago, IL, 1976, p. 282.

15 Ludwig von Mises, *Human Action: A Treatise on Economics*, 3rd edn, revised, Henry Reginery, Chicago, IL, 1966.

16 This quotation appears in Susan Cole's study, p. 58, cited above. It is from Mises, *Human Action*, pp. 248–9.

17 Israel M. Kirzner, *Competition and Entrepreneurship*, University of Chicago Press, Chicago, IL, 1973. His more recent entrepreneurial study, *Perception, Opportunity and Profit*, University of Chicago Press, Chicago, IL, 1979, has two perceptive chapters (2 and 3) dealing with the history of economic thought on entrepreneurship. These studies emphasize repeatedly his interpretation of the "... difference between 'Robbinsian' maximizing, economizing decisions and 'Misesian' human action." But he persists in his view that entrepreneurial ability has no economic value.

18　This erroneous conclusion is most clearly stated in Kirzner's paper "Alertness, Luck, and Entrepreneurial Profit," presented at the American Economic Association Meeting, August 31, 1978. It is included in his *Perception, Opportunity, and Profit* as chapter 10, see p. 181.

19　Friedman, *Price Theory*, pp. 107–9.

20　Gary S. Becker, *Economic Theory*, Knopf, New York, 1971, p. 123. In a footnote, all too brief, Becker is explicit on this point.

21　Mark Blaug, *Economic Theory in Retrospect*, 3rd edn, Cambridge University Press, Cambridge, 1978, p. 483.

6

Stationary State versus Modernization

Economic modernization may imply progress. But its income increasing consequences are seldom neutral. A stationary state implies that no increases or changes occur.[1] The economic value of human abilities to restore equilibrium in such an economic state is zero.

Long-standing unsettled social issues are being raised once again in evaluating the unwanted consequences that are attributed to the process of economic modernization. Doubts about the ultimate value of economic progress persist. Zero economic growth, coupled with zero population growth, is viewed by some people as a necessary condition of an ideal society. It could be that birth and death rates are tending toward a population equilibrium.[2] Below replacement fertility rates in industrial societies are now evident. Most people, however, act as if they prefer the increasing range of opportunities they obtain from the increases in income associated with economic modernization. This does not imply that they are unconcerned about particular adverse social effects attributed to modernization.

Intellectuals who specialize in abstract ideas differ greatly in their assessments of the value to society of a stationary state relative to that of a progressive economic state. What is at issue, as a rule, are the revealed preferences of people who are served by the economy. The economist "knows" that the preferences of people are fundamental to his analytical work.

Even if he had the courage, it would be cynical and less than candid for him to assert that the intellectuals who disagree with him are typically biased by living in sheltered affluent enclaves. But regardless of the facts on this point, an economy is supposed to serve the preferences of people, not the particular preferences of economists.

1   Long-Standing Disagreements

We start with the ideas of economic progress of the early English economists, who were not, however, of one mind about the value of what was then called the "progressive state." For Adam Smith,[3] "the progressive state is in reality the cheerful and hearty state . . ." while "the stationary state is dull." Ricardo concurred. John Stuart Mill,[4] in contemplating the progressive changes in the economy, was "not satisfied with merely tracing the laws of movement." Akin to some of the present protesters, he, too, was troubled by the ultimate purpose of these "progressive" movements. He maintained that rich and prosperous countries could derive real advantages from the stationary state. For countries to forgo these advantages meant paying too high a price for further improvements in the productive arts and for the additional accumulations of capital. Mill[5] puts it thusly:

> I am inclined to believe that it [stationary state] would be, on the whole, a considerable improvement on our present condition. I confess I am not charmed with the ideal of life held out by those who think that the normal state of human beings is that of struggling to get on; that the trampling, crushing, elbowing, and treading on each other's heels, which form the existing type of social life, are the most desirable lot of human kind, or anything but the disagreeable symptoms of one of the phases of industrial progress.

Marshall,[6] however, disagreed sharply with the eminent Mill, in these words: "But indeed a perfect adjustment is inconceivable. Perhaps even it is undesirable. For after all man is the end of production; and perfectly stable business would be likely to produce men who were little better than machines."

Judging from the economic behavior of people before and since the time of Mill, they prefer an economy with "progressive changes." Moreover, since Mill's time modern economies have developed specialized sectors, the purpose of which is to improve the productive arts. The accumulation of capital goes on apace. The economy is organized to produce a type of "progress."

2 The Two Economic States Compared

Once an economy arrives at an equilibrium and the supply of resources and the demand for services remain constant, custom could fix rents, wages, and the interest rate, and the economy would continue to be efficient.[7] Prices could be efficient as long as all economic conditions remained unchanged.

In this context it is instructive to compare the realized overall economic efficiency under stationary and progressive conditions. A simple comparison between traditional and modern agricultural conditions reveals the difference. Consider the inference that emerges before elaborating on the underlying circumstances or on the implications they have for applications of theory. The basic inference is that farm people under stationary traditional conditions are closer to an economic optimum, given the resources that are available to them, than "modern" farm people are in view of the new and better possibilities that are constantly crowding in on them. The term "farm people" is used advisedly because in this context it is not only farm production that matters, but also household production and the investment in human capital by farm people. Farm people in India, before the Green Revolution, were closer to an optimum in using the resources at their disposal than the farm people of Iowa have been since the early thirties, in view of the many complex changes in resources and associated opportunities with which they have been dealing. The reasoning underlying this inference can be stated simply. Farm people who have lived for generations with essentially the same resources tend to approximate the economic equilibrium of the stationary state. When the productive arts remain virtually constant over many years, farm people know from long experience what they can produce given the land, equipment, and their own time at work. In allocating the resources at their disposal, in choosing a combination of crops, in deciding on how and when to cultivate, plant, water, and harvest, and what combination of tools to use with draft animals and simple field equipment – these choices and decisions all embody a fine regard for marginal costs and returns. These farm people also know from experience the value of their household production possibilities in allocating their own time along with material goods within the domain of the household; again, they are finely attuned to marginal costs and returns. Furthermore, children acquire the worthwhile skills from their parents, as children have for generations under circumstances where formal schooling has little economic value. This simplified economic picture of traditional farm life, which includes knowing how to live with variations in weather, strongly implies a high level of general economic efficiency.[8] It also implies that, for all practical purposes, there is no premium for the human ability to deal with economic changes.

In contrast, farm people who live in a modernizing economy deal with sequences of changes in economic conditions which are in general not of their own making, changes originating mainly out of the activities of people other than farm people. For this reason, Schumpeter's theory of economic development is far from sufficient to explain most of these changes. The changes are nevertheless endogenous because they have their origin predominantly in the useful contributions that flow from organized agricultural research and from improvements in the inputs that farm people purchase and use in agricultural and household production. Accordingly, the *demand* for the human ability to deal with new and better production possibilities is in large part determined by organized agricultural research and by non-farm firms that produce the inputs that farm people purchase. Furthermore, it takes time to reallocate resources in arriving at a new equilibrium. Then, too, additional changes occur even before the reallocation called for by the preceding change has been completed. Hence, the implication is that "full efficiency" is kept beyond the reach of these farm people.

3   Routine and Repetitive Activity

By way of review, what human agents do in a stationary equilibrium economy is strictly routine and repetitive. No new economic decisions are required. There are no incentives to alter the prevailing routine. Production and consumption activities are repetitive. As noted above, people do what their forebears did over the life cycle. There is no reason nor incentive to search for additional information. What is known from past experience is optimal in allocating the available resources efficiently. The work that is done is repetitive. No new skills are called for. There are no changes in expectations. The rational thing to do under these conditions is to continue doing what is being done. Although people are poor, they may be illiterate, their economic life may be harsh, yet they are routinely equating their marginal utility and their marginal cost to a fine degree.

The realities that human agents face as economic conditions change are far from placid. For them routine and repetitive economic behavior is not the order of the day.

4   As Transitions Occur

The doctrine that poor people in low income countries have ironclad preferences to hold fast to their traditional production and consumption is inconsistent with well documented evidence.[9] They make the transition from the stationary state situation when better economic opportunities to improve their lot become evident. A decisive consideration is whether the new opportunities are worthwhile when the transition costs are reckoned. Thus, the incentives and the cost constraints influence the shape of the expected profitability and the responses.

There are various classes of changes in economic conditions that give rise to disequilibria. Those changes that entail small reallocations of resources imply that the transition is less difficult to achieve than it is when the changes require large reallocations. When the changes are large, the analytical difficulties for the economist mount.

When a superior high-yielding variety of grain, which requires no changes in the other factors of production and no changes in cropping practices, becomes available, the adoption of the new variety occurs readily in response to the profitability of its adoption. But when in order to be successful the new high-yielding variety requires the application of commercial fertilizer and pesticides, decidedly better control of the supply of water via irrigation, and the purchase and use of additional equipment, all of which were not required for the traditional variety that is replaced, the adoption becomes more difficult.

The distinction between changes in economic conditions that are expected to be transitory and those that are expected to be permanent implies a difference in the response on the part of human agents in dealing with these two distinct sets of changes.

Both for the human agent and for the economist in his

analytical work, changes in economic conditions that occur from within the economy proper are, as a rule, less difficult to comprehend and to deal with than are the changes in economic conditions that occur from without the economy.

To summarize, the intellectual debate pertaining to the welfare implications of the idea of economic progress compared with the idea of a stationary economic state and its welfare implications has a long history. Arguments about these ideas continue. Most people, however, act as if they prefer the increasing range of opportunities that become available to them as economic modernization occurs. Their actions reveal their decisions to forgo the routine placid economic life of a no-growth economy for the additional opportunities to improve their economic lot. Their actions also contribute importantly to restoring equilibrium.

Economic growth models that omit the restoration process are analytically inadequate. A comparison of the economic behavior of people under conditions of a stationary economic state and under conditions of economic advances tells much of the story of who it is that restores equilibrium. In telling this story, it is necessary to see clearly the transition from a repetitive to a modernizing economy. As this transition occurs, the differences in the implications of small and large changes in economic conditions matter. So do the differences in the implications of what are perceived as transitory or permanent changes. Not least is the great difficulty for human agents in reality and for economists analytically in dealing with large changes.

Notes and References

1   A part of this chapter was first presented in my "The Value of the Ability to Deal with Disequilibria," *Journal of Economic Literature*, 13, September 3, 1975, 827–46.
2   Theodore W. Schultz, "The High Value of Human Time:

Population Equilibrium," *Journal of Political Economy*, Part II, 82 (2), March–April 1974, S2–10. Kingsley Davis et al. (eds), "Below-Replacement Fertility in Industrial Societies," *Population and Development Review*, 12 (Supplement), 1986.

3   L. Robbins, "On a Certain Ambiguity in the Conception of Stationary Equilibrium," *Economic Journal*, 40, June 1930, 194–214.

4   John Stuart Mill, *Principles of Political Economy*, edited with an introduction by Sir W. J. Ashley, Longmans, Green, London, 1909, as reprinted 1926, Book IV, ch. VI.

5   In arguing for the idea of the stationary state, Mill did not anticipate that "general equilibrium theory" would become the analytical core of economics. Robbins ("On a Certain Ambiguity") makes the point that the first paragraph of Book IV of Mill's *Principles of Political Economy* opened the door for many ambiguities by his "adding a theory of motion to our theory of equilibrium. . . ." Robbins continued to hold fast to equilibrium theory and expressed the belief that it cannot be extended to cope with economic development. L. Robbins, *The Nature and Significance of Economic Science*, 2nd edn, Macmillan, London, 1935.

6   Alfred Marshall, *Industry and Trade*, Macmillan, London, 1919.

7   There are studies by anthropologists of isolated "primitive" communities that show that the rewards to the factors of production are fixed by custom.

8   This is the foundation of my analysis of the allocative efficiency of farm people in traditional agriculture in *Transforming Traditional Agriculture*, Yale University Press, New Haven, CT, 1964. The University of Chicago Press in 1983 published a paperback of this book. As a matter of historical fact, however, it would be rare indeed to discover a situation and a period during which farm people were in "perfect" equilibrium for reasons that are noted with care in *Transforming Traditional Agriculture*.

9   The evidence will be presented in later chapters.

7

Ideas and Concepts at Issue

The origins of changes in economic conditions require additional elaboration. So do the implications of the dichotomy that separates entrepreneurial earnings from true uncertainty profit or loss. We shall also explore the magnitude of entrepreneurial earnings and the elements of entrepreneurial ability. Ideally a general equilibrium theory integrates all economic elements into a consistent core. Specialization in what economists do fosters many partial theories to analyze specific activities. The theoretical possibility of the existence of an equilibrium for a competitive economy is deemed to be important for the core of general equilibrium theory.[1]

But theory is not immutable. It is susceptible to being changed by new ideas. It is being extended and applied to new problems to analyze aspects of economizing activities that had heretofore been omitted.[2] As yet, we are far from having an all-inclusive theory that encompasses all types of economic activity.

Various economic concepts are at issue because they do not correspond to observable reality. This lack of correspondence is strongly stressed by Ronald Coase[3] in his argument for his concept of the firm "which is not only realistic in that it corresponds to what is meant by a firm in the real world, but is tractable. . . ." Coase's seminal contribution is based on (a) the distinction between the economic coordination performed by market prices and the coordination performed by entrepreneurs within firms, and (b) the assumption that the firm exists because the costs of using market prices for some transactions are higher than when such transactions are organized within a firm.

Sherwin Rosen[4] extended Coase's analysis of transaction costs that are internal to firms and less costly than similar transactions carried out in markets. Rosen draws attention to the empirical content of transaction costs entailed by a firm's employment of specific human capital. He also explores the limits of labor market decentralization. His extension of the Coase "law" adds to an understanding of the limits of firms and the limits of markets.

Already in 1936 Hayek's[5] treatment of *Economics and Knowledge* made a significant contribution in regard to the role that assumptions and propositions about the knowledge possessed by different members of society play in economic analysis and the extent to which the core of equilibrium theory conveys any knowledge about what happens in the real world. His main contention is ". . . that the tautologies, of which formal equilibrium analysis in economics essentially consists, can be turned into propositions which tell us anything about causation in the real world only in so far as we are able to fill those formal propositions with definite statements about how knowledge is acquired and communicated." Hayek[6] is deeply concerned about the unbridged gap between the "Pure Logic of Choice" and what is meant by observable facts. He anticipates the unsolved question of what is deemed to be known ". . . whether the facts referred to are supposed to be given to the observing economist, or to the person whose actions he wants to explain, and if to the latter, whether it is assumed that the same facts are known to all the different persons in the system. . . ." These critical conceptual issues, as we shall show later in this chapter, are made pointedly by Lucas[7] in his business cycle studies.

1   An Equilibrating Hypothesis

Equilibrium theory is a logical abstract, an idealized economic optimum. Any disequilibrium is less. The equilibrating hypothesis asserts that when economic agents perceive they are in a state of disequilibrium, and it is possible and worthwhile to regain equilibrium, they proceed to reallocate their resources accordingly. Evidence to test this hypothesis would consist of human actions taken that have the effect of reestablishing an economic equilibrium. Like the earth's gravity which pulls in rocks and metal fragments that come near enough from outer space, there are incentives that induce entrepreneurs to reallocate their resources and in doing so to restore an economic equilibrium in their domain.

There are difficulties in testing this hypothesis, however. Disequilibria are not homogeneous because changes in economic conditions are of many types. Each disequilibrium is change specific. When a disequilibrium is small, it is difficult to observe incremental responses to the actions of economic agents. It is difficult to distinguish between some uninsurable risk and true uncertainty. Both exist in the entrepreneur's domain. The entrepreneur may be the recipient of an unforeseeable profit or loss. It is necessary to distinguish between the income that an economic agent derives from his contribution to production which he earns, and the profit or loss from true uncertainty. It is difficult to specify the data that are required and how they may be acquired to test the equilibrating hypothesis.

Beyond the limitations of theory and evidence, there are language barriers. Serious differences exist in the meaning attributed to the concepts of risk, uncertainty, profit, and entrepreneurial earnings, and also to the concepts of the origins of changes in economic conditions, and economic development, economic growth, and economic modernization. Schumpeter's idea of development and its origins once again merits special attention.

2   Origins of Changes in Economic Conditions

In Schumpeter's[8] *Theory of Economic Development*, changes
in economic conditions originate either from within or from
without the economic system. His concept of development is
as follows: "By 'development,' therefore, we shall understand
only such changes in economic life as are not forced upon it
from without but arise by its own initiative, from within."[9]
What is meant by "economic life" or by what is "forced upon
it from without" is far from clear. What is clear, however, is
that Schumpeter's concept of economic development excludes
most of the changes in economic conditions that occur during
economic modernization consisting of changes that create
disequilibria. Schumpeter's analysis is restricted to one subset
of entrepreneurs, namely to those who carry out large new
combinations of the means of production. They are the
"captains of industry." They are the economic innovators
and it is their innovations that account for Schumpeter's
economic development.

The limitations of Schumpeter's concept are as follows.

1   Most of the changes in economic conditions that
enhance productivity and that originate from within the
economy are not in Schumpeter's analytical domain. Basic
and applied research, which is an integral subsector of the
economy and which entails large expenditures, is a major
source of cost-reducing new production techniques. Technological advances are pervasive in a modernizing economy. It is true that some large corporations engage in
considerable "research and development," but so do some
small incorporated and unincorporated business entities. It
is rare, however, for small self-employed entrepreneurs,
who include vast millions of farmers, to engage in either
basic or applied research.

2   Schumpeter deals with new organizational ideas of
entrepreneurs; the applications of these ideas are in his

terminology *innovations*. They are not based on the findings of the corporation's own "research and development," nor on basic and applied research contributions from the subsector of the economy devoted to such research. Accordingly, Schumpeter's innovating entrepreneurs do not create the many new production opportunities that originate from basic and applied research. Both small and large entrepreneurs take advantage of such opportunities.

3 Investments in human capital are made by families and individuals assisted by public expenditures; in large measure these investments are not in the domain of the captains of industry, although such investments result in favorable changes in economic conditions.

4 The increases in production that occur from advances in the division of labor and in specialization made possible by extensions of the market over time are very important in economic modernization.

5 A large set of economic disequilibria occur as a consequence of political actions including wars, the destruction of structures and equipment, casualties and reparations. Some, although relatively few, economic disequilibria originate out of the vicissitudes of Nature. Schumpeter's theory of economic development excludes these and other "external" changes in economic conditions.

The idea that changes in economic conditions originate either from within or from without the economic system is attractive, but it is exceedingly difficult to analyze the complex interrelations between the "economic system" and the political and social systems of society. There are undoubtedly some specific political actions and some social constraints that can be identified and separated from conventional economic elements that are specific to economic activities.

3   Entrepreneurial Earnings Exclude "Uncertainty Outcomes"

The distinction between what is earned and what is not earned is critical. We again turn to Knight[10] for clarification. The key to Knight's thinking is his concept of true uncertainty. "It is this *true uncertainty* which ... gives the characteristic form of 'enterprise' to economic organization as a whole...."[11] Then again, "The presence of true profit, therefore, depends on absolute uncertainty...."[12] Knight argues cogently that his concept of *true uncertainty is not susceptible to measurement.*

In the preface to the re-issue of his essay Knight[13] states, "... I still find a fundamental significance in the analysis of uncertainty in the essay, and am puzzled at the insistence of many writers on treating the uncertainty of result in choice as if it were a gamble on a known mathematical chance...."

What entrepreneurs earn is amenable to marginal productivity analysis. In review, entrepreneurship entails human effort; it is a form of work. To ascertain the value of the time that is devoted to entrepreneurship, a theory of the value of human time is required. True uncertainty profits (or losses) are not earned. They are the consequences of unforeseeable events.

Entrepreneurs have expectations of what they may earn. These expectations are the incentives that motivate them to act. Events that happen about which they know nothing at the time that they make an economic decision are in the conceptual domain of *true uncertainty*. Such unknowable events have no effect on what entrepreneurs do at the time they respond to their earnings expectations. Since entrepreneurs cannot foresee true uncertainty events, we could ignore them, were it not that after such events have occurred there are income consequences. Such profits (losses) have income effects on subsequent production, consumption, and welfare.

True uncertainty is a scrupulously rigorous concept in the sense that it is beyond any consideration related to risk.[14] Risk is a wholly different economic concept. True uncertainty pertains strictly to future events that are completely unforeseeable. Since such events are unknowable, it is pointless to assume that entrepreneurs engage in search with respect to true uncertainty and it is also pointless to theorize about when unknowable events will occur.

Economists should be able to identify and measure true uncertainty profits (losses) that actually have occurred.[15] It would be useful to know their magnitude during particular periods of economic modernization. Without this knowledge, it is all too convenient to speculate and, in doing so, to overrate or underrate their economic importance.

The concept of true uncertainty becomes blurred and much confusion arises when terms such as "degree of uncertainty," or "extent of uncertainty," or "minimum amount of uncertainty" are introduced and featured. These terms appear occasionally in Knight's famous essay which may account for the fact that some economists interpret Knight's concept of uncertainty as if it were a measurable part of the expectations of entrepreneurs.

We need to go back to Hayek's concern about economic knowledge and about what is meant by observable facts. The facts at issue are those that are supposed to be given to the observing economist and to the person whose actions the economist wants to explain. But they are not necessarily the same facts. The distinction between what the economist knows and what the individual who makes the decision knows about the probabilities, here under consideration, is fundamental to Lucas's analysis. In dealing with this decision problem, the economist must separate the probability estimates that the entrepreneur uses based on empirical frequencies which both the entrepreneur and the economist observe, and which the economist can understand, from those probabilities based wholly on the entrepreneur's subjective assessment of events about which the economist knows nothing.[16]

4 *Separating Risk from Uncertainty*

The concept of risk for which insurance is purchased is not at issue. It is a cost that is readily ascertainable. A risk that an economic agent chooses to bear by means of self-insurance also entails a cost. But the cost of it is difficult for an economist to identify and measure because the human agent's perception of the risk and the means he uses to achieve his self-insurance are usually not readily observable. The concept of a risk that is deemed to be uninsurable either by the purchase of insurance or by means of self-insurance is an important form of risk identified by Lucas. Despite difficulties, the concept of risk is both necessary and useful in economic analysis.

The concept of true uncertainty, as defined in the preceding section, is beyond the perceptions and calculations of human agents at the time they decide how best to combine, coordinate, and use the resources at their disposal. If an entrepreneur has information about future events that make it possible for him to make a judgment about them, such events are not in the domain of true uncertainty. The view that there are degrees of uncertainty, or particular amounts of uncertainty, or some minimum uncertainty, assumes that such events have knowable probabilities. Since true uncertainty is unknowable, it cannot be perceived and it cannot be calculated.

The literature of economics abounds with models and studies that purport to take uncertainty into account. What is meant by uncertainty is as a rule left to the reader's imagination. It is as if what is meant were obvious, as obvious as the competitive price of a highly standardized commodity. There is a presumption in developing such models and in making such studies that uncertainties are an integral part of the expectations of human agents. But since neither entrepreneurs nor other economic agents can foresee uncertainty events, it is illogical and pointless to assume that they do.

The probabilities of various types of risk can be reckoned, but the probabilities of true uncertainty cannot be known. The risk component is a cost whatever its probability and regardless of how it may be "insured." A true uncertainty event is not a cost. It gives rise to unexpected profit or unexpected loss.

When high-yielding wheat became available to farmers in India, additional investment in tube wells and in other means to control the supply of water became profitable. Also, additional harvesting equipment, more animal or tractor power to prepare the seed bed, and fertilizer that heretofore had not been used became worthwhile. Learning how to combine and coordinate this array of new inputs entailed various types of risk. But since it was beyond the perceptions and calculations of farmers whether or not their soils and other aspects of their natural environment harbored organisms that would affect the growth and productivity of the new wheat variety adversely, these elements were in the domain of true uncertainty.

An entrepreneur who undertakes the construction of a new type of industrial plant that requires years of work before it is completed experiences various risks during its construction. These risks and the expenditures that are incurred are in principle contractual costs. The precise rate of output of such a new type of plant and the price of the product become known after the plant is completed and has been in operation, which will be some years after the commitment was made to build the plant. Here, too, there are various types of risk. If any true uncertainty events were to occur, they would have been unforeseeable.

The income effects of true uncertainty profits and losses on the distribution of income, on enterprise, and on social progress are major intellectual problems. Knight devotes two chapters to these issues.[17]

The aggregate earnings of entrepreneurs during recent economic modernization have undoubtedly been large, large enough to have been of substantial economic importance. For the US economy as a whole there are reliable data for the period since 1900 that provide strong evidence on this matter. Also, in the agricultural sector it can be seen that when the prices of purchased inputs and of farm commodities have not been distorted strong entrepreneurial incentives to modernize have prevailed.

The impressive increases in the productivity of the US economy imply that many changes in economic conditions have occurred and that these changes created large earnings expectations for many entrepreneurs. An important clue to the gains in productivity is the fact that the value of human time per hour of work increased over fivefold between 1900 and 1975 measured by the real compensation of manufacturing workers in the United States.[18] Since the mid-thirties, the increases in US agricultural productivity have occurred at a remarkably high rate. For the purpose at hand, pertinent agricultural data are decidedly better than they are for most other sectors of the economy.

The overarching consideration pertaining to the magnitude of the earnings expectations of entrepreneurs is that they have been in large measure favorable and frequently large in the economic modernization to which references have been made.

There are several reasons why economists have overlooked or neglected entrepreneurial earnings in their studies. The failure to distinguish between entrepreneurial earnings and true uncertainty profits (losses) is one of the reasons. No matter how large the unexplained increases in the rate of productivity, empirical work has failed to extend the standard production function to include the specific contribution of the entrepreneur. Then, too, there is the belief that the losses that are incurred as a consequence of uninsurable risks are offset by gains that are realized from bearing such risks. The primary reason, no doubt, is the choice of economists to seek shelter in the core of general economic equilibrium and in doing so to avoid the phenomenon of economic disequilibrium.

Leaving true uncertainty profits and losses aside, our tentative view based on the available evidence is that the economic contributions of entrepreneurs are such that their earnings are an important income component as economic modernization occurs.

The rewards for entrepreneurship which constitute the earnings of entrepreneurs are more often than not lost sight of in the controversy about the logical and exciting niceties pertaining to insurable and uninsurable risks and about whether or not economic disequilibria actually occur. The logic of an all-inclusive set of transaction costs covering all risks implies that there are no actual economic disequilibria and no earnings that are specifically entrepreneurial earnings. For economists this is a moral hazard.

5 Concept of Entrepreneurial Ability

While it is permissible to use "ability" and "capacity" of people interchangeably,[19] it is better to think of people as having abilities and of nonhuman factors as having capacities. The capacity of crop land can be increased by irrigation, drainage, lime to neutralize the acidity of the soil, and the application of fertilizers. The productive capacity of high-yielding new varieties of wheat exceeds that of some traditional varieties. Capacity, but not ability, is applicable to all nonhuman factors including machines, equipment, and structures. People, however, have abilities both innate and acquired. The acquired abilities of entrepreneurs are enhanced by schooling, health, and learning from experience.

The concept of the effects of the acquired ability to do the work of any specific occupation is here viewed as the "worker effect," which can be distinguished from the "allocative effect" of the entrepreneur's ability. Finis Welch[20] was the first to establish this distinction and to use it effectively in empirical research.

Allocative ability is a prerequisite for entrepreneurship. No matter what part of a modern economy is being investigated, we observe that many people are deliberately reallocating their resources in response to changes in economic conditions. How successful they are in their responses is in no small part determined by their "allocative ability." The ability to reallocate is not restricted to entrepreneurs who are engaged in business. People who supply labor services for hire or who are self-employed are reallocating their services in response to changes in the value of the work they do. So are housewives in devoting their time in combination with purchased goods and services in household production. Students likewise are reallocating their own time along with the educational services they purchase as they respond to changes in expected earnings, and in the value of the personal satisfactions they expect to derive from their education. Consumption opportunities are also changing, and inasmuch as pure consumption entails time, here, too, people are reallocating their own time in response to changing opportunities.[21]

Our knowledge of a person's abilities consists of inferences drawn from his performance. An ability is thus perceived as the competence and efficiency with which particular acts are performed. What a person does we treat as a service, and we consider only those services that are deemed to be both useful and scarce and therefore have some economic value. The service attributed to any ability has a time dimension; that is, a certain amount is accomplished per hour or day, in a year, or over a lifetime.

There are various classes of abilities; they include the ability (a) to learn, (b) to do useful work, (c) to play, (d) to create something, and (e) specifically for the purpose at hand, to deal with economic disequilibria. Since what is done can be observed, it is convenient to assume that observed performance is related to a specific ability. Although the various classes of abilities undoubtedly overlap and interact, it is useful to proceed with qualifications as if each class has a special set of attributes. There comes a point, however, at which this reductionist approach is misleading for it postulates the separability of abilities, whereas normal human beings possess hierarchies of integration among abilities.[22]

Much attention is given in our schools to the testing of aptitudes and intelligence; IQ tests, for example, are designed to predict school performance. There are tests to ascertain verbal and quantitative abilities, presumably to predict performance in education. Partly to limit the supply and partly to assure standards of performance, professional associations promote tests to determine who is "qualified" to practice law or medicine. The limitations and misuses of these various tests aside, their usefulness in determining economic performance is very limited.[23] Obviously, the tests are not designated for that purpose. Economists are still hard pressed in explaining the wide variance in the earnings profile of people over their lifetime. Virtually no attention has been given to the role of abilities with respect to the time spent and the satisfactions obtained from engaging in play, in creative activity, and in pure consumption, in spite of the fact that time is valuable and its economic value has been rising secularly and markedly in high income countries. Although changing economic conditions are pervasive in a modern economy, the efficiency with which people adjust to these changes has not yet become a part of standard economics. One of the reasons why this is so arises out of the analytical neglect of the equilibrating activities of human agents.[24]

Human beings, including entrepreneurs, possess both innate and acquired abilities. Although the genetic endowments matter, for reasons to be considered later, they are, with some exceptions, not featured in this study. Acquired abilities are treated as parts of the acquired stock of human capital. The available empirical research on acquired abilities of entrepreneurs is restricted predominantly to education and to its effects on their ability to reallocate the resources at their disposal in response to specific changes in economic conditions.

Notes and References

1 Gerard Debreu, "A Social Equilibrium Existence Theorem," *Proceedings of the National Academy of Sciences*, 38, 1952, 886–93; and *Theory of Value*, Wiley, New York, 1959; Kenneth J. Arrow and Gerard Debreu, "Existence of an Equilibrium for a Competitive Economy," *Econometrica*, 22 (3), 1954, 265–90; E. Roy Weintraub, "On the Existence of a Competitive Equilibrium: 1930–1954," *Journal of Economic Literature*, 21, 1983, 1–39. Weintraub closes his essay with the remark, "The equilibrium story is one in which empirical work, ideas of facts and falsification, played no role at all" (p. 37). See also Kenneth J. Arrow and F. H. Hahn, *General Competitive Analysis*, Holden-Day, San Francisco, CA, and Oliver and Boyd, Edinburgh, 1971; Darrell Duffie and Hugo Sonnenschein, "Arrow and General Equilibrium Theory," *Journal of Economic Literature*, 27 (2), June 1989, 565–98.

2 Close at hand are some recent extensions and applications. Jacob Mincer, "Investment in Human Capital and Personal Income Distribution," *Journal of Political Economy*, 66, 1958, 281–302. Gary S. Becker, "A Theory of the Allocation of Time," *Economic Journal*, 75, 1965; *Human Capital: A Theoretical and Empirical Analysis*, 2nd edn, Columbia University Press for the National Bureau of Economic Research, Columbia, OH, 1975; and "A Theory of Marriage," in his *The Economic Approach to Human Behavior*, University of Chicago Press, Chicago, IL, 1976. George Stigler, "The Economics of Information," *Journal of Political Economy*, 69, June 1961, 213–25. James J. Heckman, "Sample Selection Bias as a Specification Error," *Econometrica*, February 1979. Sherwin

Rosen, "Specialization and Human Capital," *Journal of Labor*, 1, 1983, 43–9. Robert E. Lucas, Jr, *Studies in Business-Cycle Theory*, MIT Press, Boston, MA, 1983, consisting of applications of what has become known as rational expectations. R. H. Coase, "The Nature of the Firm," *Economica, N.S.*, 4, 1937, 386–405. Not so recent, and in fact overlooked for more than two decades, M. G. Reid, *Economics of Household Production*, Wiley, New York, 1934. Robert E. Lucas, Jr, "On the Mechanics of Economic Development," *Journal of Monetary Economics*, 22, 1988, 3–42.

3 Coase, "The Nature of the Firm," p. 386.
4 Sherwin Rosen, "Transactions Costs and Internal Labor Markets," *Journal of Law, Economics and Organization*, 4 (3), Spring 1988, 49–64.
5 F. A. von Hayek, "Economics and Knowledge," his presidential address to the London Economics Club, No. 10, 1936, published in *Economica, N.S.*, 4, 1937, 33–54.
6 Ibid., p. 39.
7 Lucas, *Studies in Business-Cycle Theory*.
8 Joseph A. Schumpeter, *The Theory of Economic Development*, Harvard University Press, Cambridge, MA, 1949.
9 Ibid., p. 63.
10 Frank H. Knight, *Risk, Uncertainty, and Profit*. Re-issued by the London School of Economics and Political Science as no. 16 in their series of reprints. London. First reprinted 1933, second impression 1935.
11 Ibid., p. 232.
12 Ibid., p. 285, pp. 311–12, "... only true uncertainty ... explains profit...."
13 Ibid., p. xiv.
14 Ibid., p. 20. "It will appear that a *measurable* uncertainty, or 'risk' proper, as we shall use the term, is so far different from an *unmeasurable* one that it is not in effect an uncertainty at all. We shall accordingly restrict the term 'uncertainty' to cases of the non-quantitative type. It is this 'true' uncertainty, and not risk ... which forms the basis of a valid theory of profit...."
15 The large increase in food and feed grain prices that occurred as a consequence of the 1914–18 war resulted in large unex-

pected profits, especially for US farmers in areas that specialized in these grains and in feeding the corn. To this day the large investments in new barns, silos, grainaries, and houses made during that period stand apart as evidences of true uncertainty profit.

16 Lucas, *Studies in Business-Cycle Theory*, pp. 125, 223, and 236.

17 Ibid., chs xi and xii.

18 Based on Albert Rees's study in *Long Term Economic Growth, 1860–1970*, US Bureau of Economic Analysis, Washington, DC, 1973, and extended by the present author to include 1975 and analyzed as a part of "The Economics of the Value of Human Time," chapter 4 in his *Investing in People*, University of California Press, Berkeley, CA, 1981; see p. 65, table 7, for the data.

19 Milton Friedman in his *Price Theory*, Aldine, Chicago, IL, 1976, uses these two terms interchangeably; the "capacity of entrepreneurs" predominates.

20 Finis Welch, "Education in Production," *Journal of Political Economy*, 78, January–February 1970, 35–59.

21 This is a restatement of my first paragraph in "The Value of the Ability to Deal with Disequilibria," *Journal of Economic Literature*, 13, September 1975, 827–46.

22 The controversy in biology between those who argue for reductionism, the essence of which is the belief that all of life can be reduced to fundamental laws of physics and chemistry, and those who argue for hierarchies and integration in biological systems is instructive on this basic issue.

23 In ascertaining the value of an ability that is embodied in a person, both the psychologist and the economist are dependent upon observable acts which are assumed to be the effects of the ability being analyzed. The psychologist may thus look for cognitive ability, the knowing activity of the mind by means of which a person becomes aware of events and the manner in which he perceives them. I am looking for the ability to perceive and interpret correctly economic events, which may be a particular type of "cognitive ability."

24 Schultz, "The Value of the Ability to Deal with Disequilibria," p. 828.

8

Income-Increasing Events

The idea of increasing returns had considerable influence on the thinking of the early economists. The origins of such returns were perceived mainly as historical events, not as analytical implications derived from theory.[1] Allyn Young[2] in his "Increasing Returns and Economic Progress" made an important analytical contribution. But Young's insights and the richness of some of the earlier ideas about economic progress have been neglected. They are now being rediscovered.

It has become increasingly evident that the analytics of growth models fail to explain most of the observable increases in income. Despite these failures, the supply of such models continues to increase. It is as if economics has become locked into a state that excludes income-increasing events. To break this lock does not imply going back "... to a state of innocence before diminishing returns...."[3]

Young's paper should have sprung this lock and opened economics so that economists could pursue the sources of increases in income that have been omitted. It should have made room for changes in economic conditions that result in increases in "output" which exceed the increases in "inputs," starting with "Adam Smith's famous theorem that the division of labor depends on the extent of the market."[4] One wonders why economists have not pursued Young's approach. As noted in chapter 1, it could be that he turned economists off by asserting, "I suspect, indeed, that the apparatus which economists have built ... may stand in the way of a clear view of the more general or elementary aspects of the phenomena of increasing returns. . . ."[5]

The origins of the phenomena of increases in returns consist of events made possible in large measure by advances in knowledge that increase the quality of capital and by man-made substitutes for natural resources that reduce the drag of these resources on increases in income. Improvements in the quality of human capital are a major source of increases in income. The location density of human capital may enhance wages and salaries and the return to physical capital.

New sources of income are increasingly evident as economic modernization occurs. Some sources consist of events that occur abruptly. One such is exemplified by the 18,000 tons of high-yielding Mexican dwarf wheat seeds made available to India in 1966. The new seed was suited to the agriculture of the Punjab and to adjacent areas. The wheat-producing part of India's agriculture entered a period of rapid growth during which production rose from 11 million tons in 1966 to 46 million tons in 1984. It could be said that, had wheat farmers in India been completely indifferent to the Mexican wheat and had they continued to plant only their traditional wheat varieties, by 1984 India would have produced 35 million fewer tons of wheat. The gross value of the additional 35 million tons in 1984 may well have been about $3.5 billion.

To have received the Mexican wheat seed was for India a great economic event.

What is not elementary is that income-increasing events are not a part of the core of general equilibrium theory. When such events occur, disequilibria also occur. Within a market oriented economy, the micro economics of restoring equilibrium are responses to incentives that induce individuals and families to reallocate their resources and, in doing so, to restore equilibrium. Their contribution to production as entrepreneurs matters.

Analyses of the micro-economic-optimizing responses to

observable economic disequilibria during periods when outputs exceed inputs are a neglected part of economics. As remarked earlier, Schumpeter's[6] approach to economic development is a notable exception. His theory is based on changes in economic conditions that originate from within the economic system. These changes occur as a consequence of what a special set of entrepreneurs do, acting within that system.

Some of the pertinent ideas of economists, before growth models became popular, have a comprehensiveness that has been lost in the highly specialized parts of today's economics.

1 Ideas Before Growth Models

Above all there is the magnificent idea pertaining to the division of labor, its origin and its income-producing capacity. The economic importance of specialization is presently underrated, especially in the case of investment in specialized human capital.

The application of early ideas about the substance and scope of diminishing returns was far from clear. It was restricted to land whereas it is applicable to all factors of production. The rational producer cannot and does not try to avoid diminishing returns; he does not try to grow (Abba Lerner's[7] phrase) "... the world's food in a flower pot." What is overlooked, however, is that Ricardo's concept of land, based on "the original and indestructible powers of the soil," omits the increases in man-made productivity of agricultural land over time.

The early economists observed that agriculture is not only land specific but that land is location specific and that nature is niggardly. Their assessment of the then state of knowledge pertaining to agriculture production was in large measure correct. They could not have anticipated the development of the array of substitutes for farm land that have become available since then.

The productivity of land, which did in fact seriously limit the economic possibilities of increasing the production of food in England at that period of history, became an essential part of Malthus's theory of population. Thus, this particular dated version of static "diminishing returns" placed an indelible mark on the history of economic thought.

Lest we forget, distinguished early economists were concerned about land ownership and critical of farmers and agriculture. Smith, Ricardo, and Hume[8] viewed agriculture as an unprogressive sector. Hume accused farm people of having a predisposition to indolence. His defamation of them is terse: "A habit of indolence naturally prevails. The greater part of the land lies uncultivated. What is cultivated, yields not its utmost for want of skill and assiduity in the farmers." Smith and Ricardo saw manufacturing and commerce as progressive whereas agriculture was the sinecure of an unprogressive landed aristocracy.

Notwithstanding the notable increases in agricultural production during the period from the first edition of Marshall's[9] *Principles* (1890) to the eighth edition (1920), the preface to the eighth edition indicates that Marshall had not fully freed himself from Ricardo's static assumption and logic pertaining to the unique scarcity of farm land as a factor of production despite changes over time in economic conditions. There is then an odd jump to a growth model with no land in Harrod's[10] *Dynamic Economics*!

In a search for the sources of increases in income, what can we learn from past economic experiences? What are the benefits of extensions of markets and trade and from the interactions among division of labor, trade, and specialized physical and human capital? To what extent is it possible for nation-states to realize increases in national income from economic modernization? We are here engaged in this search.

There appears to be little room in today's models of economic growth for Adam Smith's division of labor, its origin, and its income-producing capacity. Marshall's laws of increasing returns no longer seem to be kosher. In the same vein, we have pointed to the silent treatment by economists of Allyn Young's "Increasing Returns and Economic Progress."

Part of the explanation for this neglect of so fruitful a concept surely stems from the growing technical refinement of economics, which brings with it a desire for ever greater precision in the use of terms.[11] As theory has become ever more rigorously and minutely exact, the richness of the idea of "increasing returns" has eroded. What was once a concept that evoked many different sources of additional income streams, the vaguely sensed secrets of the process of modernization, has ended up as a simple bit of arithmetic.

When a large national economy modernizes, or when a country with a small national economy takes full advantage of its trading opportunities in the large world economy, it is of course true that larger steel mills and petrochemical plants and automotive assembly lines become economically viable. But this is only a small part of the story. It stands repeating, when the sciences of biology, including plant genetics, reach a certain level, the creation of new varieties becomes a highly skilled production process tailored to the sunlight, temperature, and rainfall of a region, and also to the texture and acidity of its soil. Plants are tailored to suit the weather and soil in order to produce higher yields. Furthermore, plant breeders also alter planting, cultivation, and harvesting of the grain, so that the required crop can be more readily mechanized.

When Adam Smith perceived that the degree of specialization depends on the extent of the market, he could not have foreseen its fullest ramifications. Today we can see that it is the extent of the world market more than anything else that accounts for whole scientific disciplines and for vast cadres of technicians who specialize on improving varieties of wheat, rice, or corn. We also see reductions in the cost of transporting, refining, and using petroleum and its products. Indeed, there is only one element that unites these countless income-producing activities: in the end, they are all *cost-saving*.

It must be kept in mind that income-increasing events, which are important wellsprings of new sources of income, are excluded from general equilibrium theory. Meanwhile a substantial part of economic modernization consists of finding cheaper and better ways of doing things.

When early English economists observed increases in production by various manufacturing industries in England, they attributed a part of the additional production to increasing returns. The favorable changes in economic conditions in their day came to be known as the Industrial Revolution. As an economic process it had much in common with what is now referred to as the Green Revolution in agriculture.

Critics of the early versions of increasing returns argued that the simplistic notion of "improvements" did not suffice to explain such returns. Later critics used theory to show that monopolies would prevail. Since monopolies were not pervasive, it was argued that increasing returns were not pervasive.

Marshall[12] argued that (a) the effects of increasing returns from scale may be *external* as well as *internal*; "the part which nature plays in production shows a tendency to diminishing returns, [while] the part which man plays shows a tendency to increasing returns," that is, man's part in agriculture conforms to the law of increasing returns; and (b) "the law of increasing return may be worded thus: an increase of labour and capital leads generally to improved organization, which increases the efficiency of the work of labour and capital." In essence, "increasing return is a relation between a quantity of effort and sacrifice on the one hand, and a quantity of product on the other."

Marshall's[13] emphasis on the economic importance of health, vigor, and acquired abilities of people foreshadowed what is now human capital. His assessment of the economic value of knowledge is profound: "Knowledge is our most powerful engine of production. . . . The distinction between public and private property in knowledge . . . is of great and growing importance: in some respects of more importance than that between public and private property in material things." From Irving Fisher[14] we have an all-inclusive concept of capital which includes human capital and which in turn includes specialized human capital, an important source of increases in income.

2   Enters Economic Measurement

A series of modern studies sponsored by the National Bureau of Economic Research showed that increases in output exceeded increases in input by a wide margin. Accordingly, large productivity gains had occurred that became known as the unexplained "residual" and also as a "measure of our ignorance."[15] It is instructive to recall the ideas that were advanced and the search for explanations for the increases in measured output that exceeded the increases in measured inputs. One looks in vain for references to income-increasing events among the many proposed solutions to this puzzle. Appeals to Smith, or to Marshall, or to Allyn Young are missing.

Studies by Denison and those by Jorgenson and Griliches loomed large in this search. They clarified and improved the basic data. Denison's approach differs from that of Jorgenson and Griliches. They disagreed head-on in a series of publications that dealt with their differences with respect to measurements and explanations. As economic literature, these papers are major contributions.[16] Denison found that a substantial part of the postwar growth in national output was due to an increase in productivity; according to Jorgenson and Griliches, almost all the increase was due to increases in real factor inputs.

In my early efforts to make room in economics for human capital, I took advantage of Fisher's all-inclusive concept of capital. My first estimates appeared in "Capital Formation by Education."[17] In retrospect I was at risk to have published estimates of stocks of reproducible tangible capital and educational capital in the labor force, including on-the-job training capital.[18]

It took a lot of on-the-job experience for me to learn that the simplifying capital homogeneity assumption is a disaster for capital theory.[19] To transform the heterogeneity of various forms of measured capital, as economic modernization occurs, into a homogeneous stock of capital is beset with unknowables.

Capital is two-faced, and what these two faces tell us about economic modernization, which is a dynamic process, are, as a rule, inconsistent stories. It must be so because the cost story is a tale about sunk investments, and the other story pertains to the discounted value of the stream of services that such capital renders. The changing economy is afloat on a rough sea of capital inequalities. Differences in the rates of return and disequilibria prevail, whether the capital aggregation is in terms of factor costs or in terms of the discounted value of the lifetime services of its many parts. Nor would a catalog of all existing growth models prove that these inequalities are equalities. But why try to square the circle? If we were unable to observe these inequalities, we would have to invent them because they are the mainspring that drives economic modernization. Various sources of additional income are concealed by such aggregation.[20]

The difficult measurement problems stressed above, including estimates of the effects of scale, education, research, and disequilibria, are identified and dealt with by Griliches[21] in his agricultural productivity studies. Most of his results appear in "Research Expenditures, Education, and the Aggregate Agricultural Production Function." Griliches[22] notes that had he "assumed equilibrium and constant returns to scale, it would have begged some of the most important questions we are interested in." He found substantial economies of scale in agriculture. His results confirm the existence of disequilibria and the observed behavior reflects the producers' actions to reduce them. In the case of fertilizer, the value of the marginal product (VMP) exceeded the fertilizer price by a ratio between 3 and 5. Faced with this large disequilibrium, farmers increased their application of fertilizer at a rate of over 7.4 percent per year. This equilibrium gap (VMP/ factor price) declined from about 5 in 1949 to 2.7 in 1959.[23] There was still a substantial disequilibrium at the end of that period.

3 Elements of the Analytics

A universal all-inclusive economic growth model that has been validated by evidence does not exist. The state of theory and evidence does not suffice to comprehend and explain recent modernization in high income countries and contributes even less to what is known about the economic modernization in low income countries.

When the analytics of the origins of income-increasing events are reduced to increases in homogeneous labor and homogeneous capital, they do not explain the increases in income. However, treating the advances in technology and the accumulations of human capital as endogenous activities is a major advance. But, at this juncture, there is a need for additional thinking and better evidence. Even so, our analytical cupboard is not bare.

An advance in technology gives rise to increases in income. We know that it enhances productivity, induces specialization, is cost-saving, and is dependent on advances in knowledge. We know that at times an advance in technology occurs abruptly. We also know that technology is not a cost-free entity because it is man-made. It is endogenous. Its effects on the quality of physical and human capital require better analysis than we now have. Advances in technology are one of the major sources of more income. How much more income, where and when, await evidence and better theory.

The analytics of human capital have become increasingly important in economics. Human capital augments the value of human time. The resulting additional income induces more specialization which further increases income. Specialized human capital induces additional modernization. How much and under what conditions await analysis. Are there external effects of human capital density that can be identified? The acquired abilities of individuals and families, which are forms of human capital, augment entrepreneurial ability to restore equilibrium. Human capital accumulation is also one of the major entities in the income-increasing process.

Research and development (R&D) have become specialized parts of economics. The production and distribution of knowledge that contributes to increases in income has become an organized sector. The economics of this sector is still in its infancy.

Not least are the demand effects of increases in personal income. The specialization induced by advances in technology, human capital accumulation, and improvements in the quality of factors and product services all enhance income. The resulting increases in income in turn induce additional specialization and a further increase in income.

The state of what is known about the economics of income-increasing events consists of fragments of evidence and of particular parts of theory. Economic modernization is time specific and location specific. The necessary building blocks, consisting of evidence and theory, are not as yet at hand to fashion an all-inclusive economic model. Theorists who believe that they are about to create a universal growth model thrive on economic logic in a vacuum; there is also an empirical brigade who believe that their facts will reveal and explain the universal properties of income-increasing events.

4 *An Economic Events Approach*

Innovations, discoveries, and other increases in income episodes are economic events. Most of them are small micro events, as in the case of a farmer's increase in corn yields made possible by hybrid seed. Such events can, as a rule, be identified and measured, and their economic effects are in general ascertainable. But when increases in income are attributed to large macro events – the Industrial Revolution for example – their influence on productivity becomes exceedingly difficult to ascertain.

Disequilibria that are linked to the occurrences of increases in income are *transitory events*. While gains in productivity brought about by them are potentially lasting, the disequilibria they create are transitory. The time span of these disequilibria is observable where these events are small and occur in open-market competition. When a new discovery or technique appears, people learn that it is worthwhile to reallocate resources. Entrepreneurs respond to the expected benefits to be had, and their actions account for the transitory nature of these events. Nature is but a minor source of the events. For all practical and analytical purposes they are consequences of the activities of human beings. They may have their origin either within or outside the economic system. Those that originate from within would be included in Schumpeter's theory of economic development.

Income-increasing events have become important sources of additional income in many countries. These events tend to spawn additional income-increasing events. The economy of an increasing number of countries has a built-in capacity to create them, notably by means of organized research, R&D in general, university based science research, and investment in education and health and in the distribution of knowledge.

The idea that large increases in income occur conjures up the old ideological issue of distribution of the resulting *surplus* from an *unearned profit*. It also points up one of the limits of the axiomatic core of general economic equilibrium. These issues notwithstanding, observable income-increasing events account for measurable increases in income and welfare.

5 More on Specialization

We do not reckon the vast increases in specialization. For industry we know about the pin factory. For agriculture we blithely assume that there is nothing comparable to a pin factory. In international trade, however, specialization has long been a part of trade theory and its applications.

Agriculture is not immune to specialization and to returns from specialized human capital. Today's modern farmer is no Crusoe. Most US corn belt farm families no longer produce eggs, milk, vegetables, and fruit for home consumption. Such items are purchased. So too are the electricity, gas for fuel, telephone service, and water – not infrequently piped in from off-farm sources – paid-for services. The typical corn farmer no longer produces his own seed corn. He buys hybrid seed appropriate to his area. Production expenses consist mainly of inputs produced by industry. The production of pigs has become specialized into (a) producing breeding stock, (b) farrowing, through weaning, (c) producing feeder pigs, and lastly (d) finishing their growth into hogs to suit the market. Yet the myth persists that there is virtually no specialized physical and human capital within agriculture.

It behooves us to keep in mind Marshall's dictum that "knowledge is the most powerful engine of production." In agriculture it is truly evident from studies of the costs and returns from agricultural research.

Studies of the economic value of agricultural research have flourished following Zvi Griliches's classic Ph.D dissertation on hybrid corn, its research costs and social returns. We now know that the rates of return to expenditures on organized agricultural research in general have been and continue to be higher than the going normal rates of returns on physical capital investments.

It is noteworthy that agricultural scientists, by virtue of their acquired skills, are specialized human capital.

Scale effects on returns are well known. The contributions of human capital to farm and farm household productivity are receiving increasing attention. An important factor in the economic success of agricultural research is the specialized human capital of agricultural scientists.

Finis Welch[24] found that the value of farmers' education in production is high as agricultural modernization occurs. Welch succeeded in separating the *work effect* from the *allocative effect* of education. The favorable returns to the schooling and higher education of farmers are in large measure the result of the allocative effects of education. This acquired allocative ability functions as *a specialized form of human capital*.

Specialization abounds in our cities and factories, in commerce, manufacturing, and in light and heavy industries. But what about the professions? I turn to the production and distribution of knowledge in the United States based on the studies by Machlup.[25] His 1962 book is rich on the vast extent of the specialization that prevails. The last book from Machlup's[26] fertile mind is on the economics of information and human capital within the core of economics. The extent and complexity of the knowledge-producing professions bespeak *human capital specialization* and it accounts in good measure for much of their productivity.

Specialization, however, has its limits. It, too, is subject to diminishing returns. Hayek's[27] "Dilemma of Specialization" exists. There are losses from over-specialization. Not to be concealed is the fact that economists are also vulnerable to over-specialization.

6 *Additional Analytics and Evidence*

Trade effects of human capital on the composition of the goods that are traded account for the Leontief *paradox*, which asserts that, contrary to trade theory, capital-rich countries export labor intensive goods. We now know that the labor services entering into such goods are human capital intensive. A capital-rich country exports the services of specialized human capital.

In his *Treatise on the Family*, Becker[28] compares his analysis with the division of labor within the household to that which occurs in international trade. Members of the household specialize their investments and time. "Moreover, with constant or increasing returns to scale, *all* members of efficient households must be completely specialized." Becker[29] returns to his argument that increasing returns from specialized human capital are a strong force creating a division of labor in the allocation of time and investments in human capital between married men and married women.

Two-way trade in similar products between similar countries has been further explored by Daniel Gros.[30] He argues that increasing returns made possible by specific human capital specialization explain a particular class of trade. In an in-depth analysis of physicians' services and the division of labor across local markets, James R. Baumgardner[31] found that micro-level evidence "indicates that specialization occurs at an even finer level than can be demonstrated at aggregate level."

Rosen[32] came to the issues at hand in his "Substitutions and Human Capital" and then in "Specialization and Human Capital" with the following telling argument:

> Incentives for specialization, trade, and the production of comparative advantage through investment are shown to arise from increasing returns to utilization. Hence, the rate of return is increasing in utilization and is maximized by utilizing specialized skills as intensively as possible. Identically endowed individuals have incentives to specialize their investments in skills and trade with each other for this reason, even if production technology exhibits constant returns to scale. The enormous productivity and complexity of modern economies are in good measure attributable to specialization.

Lucas[33] in his Marshall Lectures, "On the Mechanics of

Economic Development," focuses on physical and human capital accumulation interactions and on systems that admit specialized human capital. Lucas assigns a role to the *external effects* of human capital. These effects spill over from one person to another, people at each skill level are more productive in high human capital environments, and human capital enhances the productivity of both labor and physical capital. Evidences in support of such external effects are not as yet at hand.

Lucas sees "human capital accumulation as a *social* activity, involving *groups* of people, in a way that has no counterpart in the accumulation of physical capital."

A country's human capital at any given date is an important economic fact in analyzing the production possibilities of the country. The productivity value of this human capital "endowment" depends in large part on its composition in relation to market opportunities for the services of each part of the composition. What matters in this context is the heterogeneity of human capital. In labor economics the distinction between general human capital and firm-specific human capital of workers in the firm is useful analytically. The concept of specialized human capital encompasses a large number of forms of human capital that pertain to income-increasing events.

7 *Can Income-Increasing Events be Attained by Rational Investments?*

Is it possible to anticipate particular forms of specialized human capital that have a high probability of generating income-increasing opportunities which would warrant investment? It can be done and it is being done.

In large measure, expenditures on R&D qualify. Broadly defined, R&D are major sources of technical advances originating out of basic and applied research which entail specialized human capital. Thus R&D scientists develop new and better techniques for production, the applications of which give rise to increases in income. Organized agricultural research throughout the world has become a sizable subsector of the economy with annual expenditures equivalent to about $8 billion during the mid-eighties. At the micro level, the acquired scientific ability of a top flight geneticist who devotes his research to increasing the productivity of plants (crops) is instructive. He is an essential spoke in the organized agricultural research wheel that has increased greatly the food-producing capacity of agriculture. The prospects are that this important source of gains in agricultural productivity is still far from having been exhausted.

Another class of investment in specialized human capital that results in income increases over the life span of human beings is exemplified by investment in primary schooling. What is at stake is the acquired ability to have mastered a language sufficiently to *read* efficiently and to *write* with competence.[34] Here, too, marked advances have been achieved in many low income countries since the Second World War measured by increases in primary schooling.[35] There is a large body of evidence which shows that, in countries where agriculture is being modernized, the rate of returns to the primary schooling of farmers is high.

8 Concluding Remarks

Specialized human capital is an important source of income increases. Growth theory that excludes the formation of such human capital is far from adequate. Growth theory that excludes the income contributions of entrepreneurs is also inadequate. Understanding the interdependence of these two phenomena is crucial in explaining modernization experience. On various important issues pertaining to economic progress early economists had comprehensive insights that growth models omit. Smith's division of labor, made possible by specialization constrained by the extent of the market, is a fundamental insight. So are Marshall's "laws" of increasing returns. What is hard to explain is the long neglect on the part of economists of Young's classic paper. During the era of the puzzle of the residual, economic measurement was unencumbered by Smith, or Marshall, or Young.

There are indications that endogenous advances in technology, increases in the quantity and quality of human capital, and specialization are on the research agenda of a number of economists.[36] Our myopic view of economic modernization is being corrected by appropriate lenses.

Notes and References

1 A part of this chapter is based on my Yale lecture, "On Investing in Specialized Human Capital to Attain Increasing Returns," in *The State of Development Economics*, edited by Gustev Ranis and T. Paul Schultz, Basil Blackwell, London, New York, 1988. I am indebted to Zvi Griliches on the residual issue; James Heckman on the state of the evidence; Robert Lucas on specialized human capital; Sherwin Rosen on the intensive utilization issue; George Tolley on externalities in cities; Jacob Frenkel on trade studies; Lester Telser on innovation theory; George Stigler on theory in retrospect; T. Paul Schultz on Schumpeter on disequilibria; John Letiche on the growing literature on issues in international economics; and Richard Barichello for helpful suggestions. In note 11 I indicate my debt to A. C. Harberger for his clarification of my argument in the publication set forth in note 11.

2 Allyn A. Young, "Increasing Returns and Economic Progress," *Economic Journal*, December 1928, 527–42.

3 This phrase is from Hicks, *Capital and Growth*, Oxford University Press, Oxford, 1965, p. 134.

4 Young, "Increasing Returns," p. 529.

5 Ibid., p. 527.

6 Joseph A. Schumpeter, *The Theory of Economic Development*, Harvard University Press, Cambridge, MA, 1949. Also, *Capitalism, Socialism and Democracy*, Harper and Brothers, New York, 1942, ch. XII.

7   Abba Lerner, *The Economics of Control*, Macmillan, New York, 1941, p. 161.

8   David Hume, *Writing on Economics*, edited by Eugene Rotwein, University of Wisconsin Press, Madison, WI, 1955, p. 10. I am indebted to Nathan Rosenberg on this point.

9   Alfred Marshall, *Principles of Economics*, Macmillan, London, 1960. In the preface of the eighth edition, dated October 1920, pp. xv–xvi, the following paragraph appears:

> There have been stages in social history in which the special features of the income yielded by the ownership of land have dominated human relations: and perhaps they may again assert a pre-eminence. But in the present age, the opening out of new countries, aided by low transport charges on land and sea, has almost suspended the tendency to Diminishing Return, in that sense in which the term was used by Malthus and Ricardo, when the English labourers' weekly wages were often less than the price of half a bushel of good wheat. And yet, if the growth of population should continue for very long even at a quarter of its present rate, the aggregate rental values of land for all its uses (assumed to be as free as now from restraint by public authority) may again exceed the aggregate of incomes derived from all other forms of material property; even though that may then embody twenty times as much labor as now.

10 R. F. Harrod, *Towards a Dynamic Economics*, Macmillan, London, 1948, p. 20.

11 This section is based on a part of my "The Long View in Economic Policy: The Case of Agriculture and Food," published by the International Center for Economic Growth, San Francisco, CA, 1987. Here I am indebted to A. C. Harberger for clarifying aspects of the ideas pertaining to increasing returns.

12 Marshall, *Principles of Economics*, Book IV, ch. xiii, p. 318.

13 Ibid., Book IV, "The Agents of Production," ch. 1, pp. 138 and 193.

14 Irving Fisher, *The Nature of Capital and Income*, Macmillan, New York, London, 1906.

15 Moses Abramovitz, "Resource and Output Trends in the United States Since 1890," *Occasional Paper 52*, National Bureau of Economic Research, New York, 1956, 23 pages.

Solomon Fabricant, "Basic Facts on Productivity Change," *Occasional Paper 63*, National Bureau of Economic Research, New York, 1959, 49 pages.

16 Five of the principal publications on these issues appear in US Department of Commerce publication *Survey of Current Business, The Measurement of Productivity*, Part II, May 1972, vol. 52, no. 5, pp. 1–111 on p. 1. It is also available as Reprint 244 of the Brookings Institution, Washington, DC.

17 Theodore W. Schultz, "Capital Formation by Education," *Journal of Political Economy*, 68, December 1960, 571–83.

18 Theodore W. Schultz, "Reflections on Investment in Man," *Journal of Political Economy*, 70 (Supplement), October 1962, 1–8.

19 John Hicks, *Capital and Growth*, Oxford University Press, Oxford, 1965, p. 35.

20 Theodore W. Schultz, "Human Capital: Policy Issues and Research Opportunities," in *Human Resources*, National Bureau of Economic Research, New York, 1972, pp. 1–84.

21 Zvi Griliches, "Research Expenditures, Education, and the Aggregate Agricultural Production Function," *American Economic Review*, December 1964, 961–74; "Specification and Estimation of Agricultural Production Functions," *Journal of Farm Economics*, May 1963; and "The Sources of Measured Productivity Growth: United States Agriculture, 1940–1960," *Journal of Political Economy*, August 1963, 331–46.

22 Griliches, "Specification and Estimation."

23 Griliches, "Research Expenditures."

24 Finis Welch, "Education in Production," *Journal of Political Economy*, 78, 1970, 35–59.

25 Fritz Machlup, *The Production and Distribution of Knowledge in the United States*, Princeton University Press, Princeton, NJ, 1962, xix and 416 pages; *Knowledge and Knowledge Production*, Princeton University Press, Princeton, NJ, 1980, xxix and 272 pages; and *The Branches of Learning*, Princeton University Press, Princeton, NJ, 1982, xii and 205 pages.

26 Fritz Machlup, *The Economics of Information and Human Capital*, Princeton University Press, Princeton, NJ, 1984, xvi and 644 pages and foreword and introduction.

27 F. A. Hayek, "The Dilemma of Specialization," in *The State of*

the Social Sciences, edited by Lenard D. White, University of Chicago Press, Chicago, IL, 1956, p. 463.

28 Gary S. Becker, *A Treatise on the Family*, Harvard University Press, Cambridge, MA, 1981, pp. 20–1.

29 Gary S. Becker, "Human Capital, Effort, and the Sexual Division of Labor," *Journal of Labor Economics*, 3 (1), 1985, 533–58.

30 Daniel Gros, "Increasing Returns and Human Capital in International Trade," Ph.D. Disseration, University of Chicago, 1984.

31 James R. Baumgardner, "Physicians' Services and the Division of Labor Across Markets," *Journal of Political Economy*, 96, October 1988, 948–82.

32 Sherwin Rosen, "Substitution and Division of Labor," *Econometrica*, 45 (1), 1976, 861–8; and "Specialization and Human Capital," *Journal of Labor Economics*, 1, 1983, 43–9.

33 Robert E. Lucas, Jr, "On the Mechanics of Economic Development," his Marshall Lecture, Cambridge University, May 1985, in *Journal of Monetary Economics*, 22, 1988, 3–42.

34 Mark Rosenzweig comments "On Investing in Specialized Human Capital to Attain Increasing Returns," in *The State of Development Economics*, edited by Gustav Ranis and T. Paul Schultz, Basil Blackwell, Oxford, 1988, pp. 354–6. He treats language as a form of human capital as a means of attaining increasing returns.

35 T. Paul Schultz, "Education Investments and Returns in Economic Development," Economic Growth Center, Yale University, Paper 528, February 1987.

36 Paul M. Romer, "Dynamic Competitive Equilibria with Externalities, Increasing Returns and Unbounded Growth," Ph.D. Dissertation, University of Chicago, 1983. For the extensive growing literature on these issues in international economics, see the references cited in Elhanan Helpman and Paul R. Krugman, *Market Structure and Foreign Trade: Increasing Returns, Imperfect Competition, and the International Economy*, MIT Press, Boston, MA, 1985; Avinash Dixit, "Strategic Aspects of Trade Policy," paper delivered at the Fifth World Congress of the Econometric Society, September 1985 (forthcoming); R. W. Jones and P. B. Kenen (eds), *Hand-*

book of International Economics, North-Holland, Amsterdam, 1984. Recent unpublished papers since this chapter was completed: Mark R. Rosenzweig, "Population Growth and Human Capital Investment," University of Minnesota, 1988; Paul R. Krugman, "Endogenous Innovations, International Trade and Growth," May 1988; Paul M. Romer, "Endogenous Technological Change," May 1988; Robert J. Barro, "Government Spending in a Simple Model of Endogenous Growth," Harvard University, 1988; S. C. Tsiang, "Success or Failure in Economic Takeoff," Chung-Hua Institution for Economic Research, 1988; Paul M. Romer, "Increasing Returns, Specialization, and External Economics: Growth as Described by Allyn Young," University of Rochester, Conferences on Human Capital and Economic Growth, 1988 and 1989, awaiting publication.

9

Demand and Supply of Entrepreneurs

People have both innate and acquired entrepreneurial abilities. The acquired part is enhanced by experience, on-the-job training, schooling, education, and improvements in health. Each of these is an investment in human capital. The potential supply of acquired abilities is large. Innate abilities are inherited.

To what extent is the existing supply of abilities actually used during the process of modernization? Much depends on the demand. There is no steady stable demand for entrepreneurial ability as economic conditions change during modernization. Moreover, no person is only an entrepreneur in his economic activities. Being an entrepreneur is not a full-time endeavor. But how much time[1] during any given day or year that is devoted to allocative decisions is a critical unsettled issue.

As noted earlier, entrepreneurs are not accorded the status of an occupation. There are no entrepreneurial statistics. Reported wages, salaries, and other earnings for work do not give us entrepreneurial earnings. What entrepreneurs earn is not identified in national income accounting. Nor are their earnings identified in micro studies that use standard production function techniques. These studies may report a residual, but the part of the residual that was earned by the entrepreneur is left undetermined.

Our primary concern is to understand the economic function of entrepreneurs in dealing with changes in economic conditions in a modernizing economy. We do not feature the coordination of the factors of production within the firm as Coase[2] has done: a market economy under his equilibrium assumption.

We seek to explain the behavior of entrepreneurs in a modernizing economy that is not in a state of equilibrium. Our approach concentrates on the demand for and supply of the services of entrepreneurs when disequilibria prevail. Although it is more difficult to ascertain the demand for the services of entrepreneurs than that of the supply, we begin with the demand. Whereas the literature of economics is rich in studies of demands, there are none for the services of entrepreneurs.

1 Elements of the Demand

What an entrepreneur expects to "earn" for his allocative effort is the incentive that motivates his actions. The incentive depends in part on the expected transitory nature of the income to be derived from equilibrating actions. It is this expected entrepreneurial income that induces the economic agent to enter upon the equilibrating activities. As a process it is exemplified by the profitability of the adoption of hybrid corn. In household production it is exemplified by the benefits derived from the adoption of refrigerators. It is also evident where laborers migrate to better jobs. College students endeavor to improve their expected earnings by adjusting their studies to changes in the market for educated personnel. By these actions farmers, housewives, laborers, and students, at the time and under the implied economic conditions, are entrepreneurs responding to changes in opportunities.

For a given disequilibrium, it is helpful to think of a demand schedule where the incentive to act is highest at the outset and as resources are reallocated the incentive declines. The part of this demand schedule that matters in analyzing observable behavior lies substantially above a zero gain. When the additional gain becomes too small the incentive becomes too weak to warrant proceeding to the "perfect" equilibrium point. The disequilibrium associated with the event of hybrid corn is instructive. Hybrid corn became available in the early thirties and it spread rapidly throughout the Corn Belt. There were marked geographic differences, however, in the rate at which it was adopted. These differences in the rate of adoption were a consequence of the wide differences in the profitability from the increases in yield that could be obtained from the available hybrid seed. In Iowa in four years the percentage of the total acreage planted to hybrid seed increased from 10 to 90 percent, whereas in Wisconsin during the same period it reached the 60 percent level.

The demand for what entrepreneurs do has several additional attributes. It often occurs abruptly. It is a transitory source of income and it is specific to each type of change in economic conditions. Compared with the demand for food which is relatively stable over time, in the sense that shifts in the demand and changes in its elasticity occur as a rule gradually over time, the demand for the services of entrepreneurs frequently emerges abruptly. It is transitory because it is eliminated as soon as an economic equilibrium has been restored.

As related in the preceding chapter, the demand for farm entrepreneurship in producing wheat occurred abruptly and dramatically in India when 18,000 tons of dwarf high-yielding wheat seed arrived in India from Mexico in 1966.[3]

Griliches's[4] pioneering study shows that the rate at which hybrid corn was adopted is explained by "expected profitability." In Iowa, as mentioned, it took only four years to go from 10 to 90 percent of the corn acreage planted with hybrid seed.[5] It soon reached virtually 100 percent. "In areas where the profitability was lower, the adoption was also slower."[6] The transitory nature of the expected profitability became evident when the equilibrium level of the use of hybrid seed was attained.[7]

When disequilibria occur in a public sector of an economy, the official agency is slower in restoring equilibrium within its sector than micro entrepreneurs are in their private domain.

Although official agencies respond more slowly to disequilibria than private entrepreneurs, official agencies are not immune to the adverse effects of income losses that could be reduced by resorting equilibrium in their domain. When such losses become large, official actions may be taken to reduce them. A case in point occurred when OPEC abruptly imposed large increases in the price of oil. The governments of Japan and the United States both promptly imposed controls to keep the domestic price of oil from rising on equity grounds to protect consumers. In Japan, none of the costs of this policy could be shifted to the domestic producers of oil since all oil had to be imported. The economic losses caused by the low internal oil prices were soon perceived as too high a price to pay for the equity objective. The government of Japan then shifted to pricing all oil used in Japan consistently with the price paid for imported oil. In the United States a substantial part of the cost burden of protecting consumers was shifted to domestic producers of oil. The US government persisted for years in under-pricing oil within the US economy.

A classic case of an inordinate delay on the part of an agency of government occurred when the British Admiralty did not act to eradicate scurvy after the remedy was known. In the conquest of this horrible disease, "The villain is the Admiralty of the British navy; the hero is Dr. James Lind, a Scottish physician."[8] Herbert Spencer deplored the long delay of officials in his comment, "Thus two centuries after the remedy was known, and forty years after the chief medical officer of the government had given conclusive evidence of its worth, the Admiralty, forced thereto by an exacerbation of the evil, first moved in the matter."

When economic conditions change, those entrepreneurs

who are among the first to respond successfully benefit most. In the event that the change results in a reduction in real costs, those entrepreneurs who fail to adjust to the change in economic conditions experience losses, and over time may be eliminated by competition.

In a market economy, the demand selects superior entrepreneurs in terms of their ability to deal with disequilibria, as George Tolley[9] has shown in the case of US agriculture.

2   *Elements of the Supply*

Like intelligence, entrepreneurial ability is one of the general attributes of the human population. Observable human behavior in response to changes in economic conditions indicates that most people do what is here deemed to be entrepreneurship. They break their routine and proceed to reallocate their own time and related resources when they perceive that it is worthwhile to do so. The implication is that not only individuals who are in charge of business firms but also farmers, others who are in self-employed occupations, employed workers, students, and women who are in charge of households have entrepreneurial abilities. But they differ for reasons of differences in their genetic abilities and in their acquired abilities.

In his analysis of changes in the production function, Becker[10] is correct in stating, "As conditions improve – as knowledge expands – the function 'shifts' and a larger useful output is obtainable from the same inputs. Even at a moment of time, the functions vary . . . as 'entrepreneurial' knowledge and the nature of the product vary." Furthermore, "The level of technology varies . . . among firms in the same industry because of differences in entrepreneurial ability. . . ."[11] The entrepreneur's stock of knowledge in this context is a proxy for his ability.

In accounting terms, the aggregate supply of entrepreneurship is the sum of how many adults are actually and potentially active entrepreneurs and of the quality of their genetic abilities and their acquired abilities. The supply is large in terms of numbers and the supply is widely distributed throughout the adult population at any given date. The quality of the supply is enhanced over time by investment in various forms of human capital. Such investments in human capital in response to increases in the demand for entrepreneurial abilities are complex and difficult to identify and measure. Even so, the required empirical work is being done.

As already noted, small poor illiterate farmers in low income countries have a substantial measure of entrepreneurial ability, contrary to widely held beliefs. The available supply of this ability is not restricted to Schumpeter's captains of industry, nor to successful innovators regardless of the size of firms.

Although the genetic abilities of entrepreneurs vary and the differences in abilities on this score may matter,[12] we shall concentrate on acquired abilities because, as far as we know, the distributions of genetic abilities within large populations are about the same. Thus, it is plausible that there is no appreciable difference in the level and distribution of genetic abilities between the people of China and the people of the United States. But the per capita acquired abilities are decidedly less in China than in the United States.

For individuals in a market regime, for any past or present date, there is a supply of entrepreneurial ability. Each individual has his own "private" supply curve which declines initially, as Becker has noted, ". . . because of the fixed cost of using the entrepreneur's own time and related resources. Eventually, it rises . . . because the opportunity cost of a single owner's time increases as he is forced to draw more and more on leisure and sleeping time. . . ."[13] Full-time entrepreneurship, however, is exceedingly rare. For a given day, maybe; for all of an entire year, no.

To review, the supply of acquired abilities is enhanced by experience, education, and health, each of which entails investment in human capital. As is the case in increasing the stock of any form of capital, its value changes with the shifting economic sands over time. The value of entrepreneurial capital is subject to capital heterogeneity.[14] In analyzing the effects of investment in education and of experience and health on entrepreneurial ability, each increment of such human capital must be viewed and treated as economic change specific.

3 Education and Entrepreneurship

Studies of the productivity of US agriculture provide strong evidence that education enhances the entrepreneurial ability of farmers. The empirical results are not restricted to a difference in the effects of eight and 12 years of schooling on the allocative ability of farmers. The evidence also resolves the puzzle why the proportion of US farmers with a college education is increasing. Farmers are normally both self-employed workers and entrepreneurs. Thus, the productivity effects of education are of two parts: namely, on work skills and on entrepreneurship in dealing with the disequilibria that occur as a consequence of changes in the economy.

In *Transforming Traditional Agriculture*, I advanced the hypothesis that the schooling of farmers increases their allocative ability. This hypothesis has led to many studies to determine the effects of schooling on the rate of adoption of new superior agricultural inputs. Chandhri[15] was among the vanguard in showing that changes made in the composition of agricultural inputs is sensitive to the schooling of farmers. Research in this area owes much to Welch,[16] Griliches,[17] and Evenson.[18] In Welch's approach, the demand for entrepreneurship is estimated by the level of agricultural research activity. The higher the research level, the larger the increases in production opportunities and the larger the advantages of the entrepreneurial ability acquired from education. Although the increases in productivity from the new technologies called for more work skills, it was not plausible that such additional skills of college graduates could account for all the very considerable increases in their earnings, which in Welch's study came to 62 percent more for the college graduates than for thóse who completed high school. He found that the advances in agricultural research explained roughly one-third of this difference between college and high school graduates.[19]

Huffman's studies[20] got at the heart of the allocation issue. He focused on the use of a single input, nitrogenous fertilizer,[21] in the production of corn. His rationale is that where a major economic change occurs with various lesser changes in its wake, the education of farmers should increase the rate of the adjustments. The major economic change was the 22–25 percent decline in the price of nitrogen relative to that of corn. Using a sample of county data drawn from five key corn belt states for the period 1950–4 to 1964, Huffman found that one additional year of schooling resulted in farmers earning $52 more from this one dimension of improved allocative efficiency (using nitrogen in corn production) in one farm activity.

Petzel's[22] study deals with the relationships between the education of farmers and the dynamics of acreage allocations to soybean production in the United States. His optimizing model is based on the dependence of supply on expected price. His study focuses on a period of rapid growth in the acreage devoted to soybeans in nine states from 1948 to 1973. Petzel found that the adjustments made by farmers occurred more rapidly in the counties where average education levels were highest. He also found more rapid adjustments with respect to two dimensions of scale: namely, the total crop area devoted to soybeans, and the unit scale per farm. Welch's[23] and other studies provide strong evidence on this question.

There are few economic propositions that are as valid empirically as is the proposition that the entrepreneurial ability of farmers is enhanced by their education. For low income countries we have a competent survey of the effects of education of farmers on their performance in the process of modernization of agriculture by Marlaine E. Lockheed, Dean T. Jamison, and Lawrence J. Lau.[24] Their results for each of their 20 low income countries lead them to conclude ". . . that the effectiveness of education is enhanced in a modernizing environment."[25]

The documentation of the survey cited above, including methods of analysis, data sets, treatment of education and profitability, adoption of technical advances, and rate of return to rural education, is the substance of a comprehensive book by Jamison and Lau.[26]

Entrepreneurship, however, continues to be underrated in the case of small firms and households. Increases in the supply of food entail the entrepreneurship of countless millions of small farmers. Even more millions of household entrepreneurs are involved in modernization of households. Changes in economic conditions that enhance the economic opportunities of farmers and housewives create the incentives and the demands for entrepreneurship. It is a serious omission to exclude all these small entrepreneurs as if entrepreneurship were confined to the domain of large corporations.

4   Separating Management from Entrepreneurship

The research endeavors of Edwin F. Gay, Arthur H. Cole, and Leland H. Jenks to separate management and entrepreneurship of large business firms are well known. But according to Thomas C. Cochrane,[27] their studies were not successful. It is difficult to separate these two functions. Large complex firms require more managerial ability than less complex small firms. The management of many large firms is divided among a number of managers and each manager has authority and responsibility in the domain assigned to him.

The metaphor of a team has not been fruitful.

Sherwin Rosen[28] has presented "... a theory of the joint distribution of firm size and managerial reward generated by market assignments of personnel to hierarchical positions in firms." His theory has the analytical merit that authority, control, and managerial incomes are determined by the market. In his hierarchical approach the market assigns "... persons of superior talent to top positions" which "increases productivity by more than the increment of their ability because greater talent filters through the entire firm by a recursive chain of command technology."

The implications of Rosen's theory pave the way for promising research endeavors. However, since the objective of the theory is restricted to the economic value of hierarchical management positions *under equilibrium conditions*, important as that objective is, the theory is by design not intended to determine the value of what entrepreneurs do when disequilibria occur during economic modernization.

5   Specialization

Where people are free to choose, they strive to acquire abilities that will give them the optimum utility they expect to derive from future earnings constrained by the resources at their disposal. Acquired abilities are of many different types. The greater the division of labor and specialization of economic activities, the greater the number of different types of skills there are to choose from. In chapter 8, we drew heavily on Sherwin Rosen's[29] "Specialization and Human Capital" in which he argues the case for diversity of specialized skills. Incentives for specialization, trade, and production consistent with comparative advantage through investment are shown to arise from increasing returns to the utilization of human capital. There is also specialization in entrepreneurial abilities. It is useful in thinking about the economics of human capital of entrepreneurs to distinguish between general and specific human capital.

Every adult who is an active economic agent, no matter how specialized his work may be, has various abilities that are not specific to his specialized work. A druggist who is qualified in pharmacology has acquired the expertise and credentials to operate a drugstore. Presumably he earns a satisfactory return on his investment in his specialized abilities and on the physical capital in his drugstore as he proceeds to do what druggists do routinely and repetitively. But when his economic environment changes, his response is that of an entrepreneur.[30] In the analysis of entrepreneurship, no able-bodied adult has only entrepreneurial abilities. The notion that entrepreneurs are only entrepreneurs is pure fiction.

A human being's stock of entrepreneurial ability cannot be separated from the person who has it. Viewed as a stock, it cannot be sold to someone else and it cannot be transferred to heirs. The heirs of fathers who are successful entrepreneurs are, as a rule, not up to their fathers' achievements, genetic endowment notwithstanding. A person's stock of entrepreneurial ability cannot be appropriated by governments. Jews and other ethnic groups facing the danger of being expelled have known this fact for ages. Since their physical property has often been confiscated, one of their responses has been to invest more in their human capital, including more entrepreneurial ability than they otherwise would have. So, too, have the Chinese in countries in other parts of Asia, Indians in Africa, Parsees in Bombay, Lebanese in the Middle East, Jews in Europe, and Huguenots in France.[31]

6   A Long View of Supply

In a short view, more precisely any day, the supply of entrepreneurial ability can be augmented somewhat by reducing time for leisure. What is more important in a modernizing economy are the possibilities of increasing the supply over time. Increases in entrepreneurial incentives induce investments that increase the supply. Much depends, however, on our empirical knowledge of the nature of these investment possibilities.

Learning from experience accounts for a good deal of the observable increases in entrepreneurial abilities. Such learning occurs when people are confronted by changes in economic conditions. In the case of farmers in low income countries who have little or no schooling, their observed performance reveals considerable ability to learn, to wit, in their success in the adoptions of new high-yielding grain varieties. Learning from experience is specific to producing a type of steel or a class of textiles. It is specific to producing rice or wheat, or specific to the household production of a nuclear or an extended family. Entrepreneurial abilities acquired in dealing with a particular change in economic conditions are not necessarily the required abilities to cope with a different future change in economic conditions.

The comparative advantage of the schoolroom in acquiring various abilities, including entrepreneurial abilities, depends in large measure on the complexities of the economic conditions. As technology becomes more complex, the comparative advantage of schooling and higher education over that of learning from experience increases. The economic value of education is well documented as the modernization of agriculture occurs. When the effects of experience or education on entrepreneurship are being analyzed and when the human agent deals with a once and for all improved technology, the effects are exhausted when the new equilibrium has been attained. In the event that another and different technology then becomes available, the ability that has been acquired may be rendered obsolete. Finis Welch[32] has put this aspect of technical change thusly: "A rapid rate of technical change renders past experience obsolete and it increases the informational content of today's experience. But, just as more rapid technical change renders yesterday's less relevant from today's perspective, it renders today less relevant from tomorrow's perspective."

One implication is that no general statements are possible about the value of the entrepreneurial ability unless the attributes of the changes are specified. Another implication is that the comparative advantage of schooling rises relative to that of learning from experience as technology becomes more complex and as a consequence of increases in specialization. Improvements in health that account for the observed increases in life span increase the incentives to invest in human capital.[33] A part of this increase in the stock of human capital contributes to the entrepreneurial abilities.

Thus, experience, education, and health go hand in hand. To comprehend and gauge the supply of entrepreneurs it is important to see the complementarity among them.

7   Interacting Demand and Supply – An Overview

Dana Dalrymple's[34] studies of the spread of the high-yielding wheat and rice varieties throughout many low income countries present a large view of the interacting demand and supply of entrepreneurship in the modernization of wheat and rice production.

Wheat and rice are the world's predominant food grains. Plant breeders have greatly increased the genetic capacity of these grains.

In wheat CIMMYT,[35] in Mexico, released a variety in 1950 with a yield potential of 3,000 kg per hectare of land. A better yielding variety was released in 1964; its yield potential was 6,000 kg per hectare. By 1985, 30 different varieties had been released and potential yields of 8,000 kg per hectare were attainable.[36]

In India, the test trials harvested in 1964 showed that the two Mexican semidwarf wheat varieties, Sonora 64 and Lerma Rojo 64, out-yielded all Indian control varieties by 30 percent. Norman Borlaug's mission on wheat for India helped set the stage for India's importation of 18,000 tons of the new Mexican wheat.[37]

During 1966–7, the first complete crop year for the new varieties in India, 541,000 hectares were sown to the high-yielding Mexican variety. The high-yielding variety required fertilizer and other complementary inputs. The supplies of these were inadequate and costly. Furthermore, the government procurement prices of wheat were distorted. But despite these and still other constraints, the new variety spread rapidly. By 1982–3 over 18 million hectares were sown to the high-yielding variety.[38] Wheat production in India increased from 11 million tons in the mid-sixties to 44 million tons in the early eighties. India replaced Canada as the fourth largest world producer of wheat. In 1965, India imported over 7.5 million tons of wheat. In the mid-eighties, stocks exceeded storage capacity and some wheat was exported.

The world area sown with high-yielding varieties of wheat in 1982–3 by regions in hectares had reached the millions: Asia 25.4, Near East 7.6, Africa 0.5, Latin America 8.3, and Communist Asia 8.9: a total of 50,700,000 hectares.[39]

The rapid adoption of high-yielding rice varieties has also been remarkable, specifically 77,600,000 hectares by 1982–3, and at that date 45 percent of the rice area was devoted to high-yielding varieties; in wheat the comparable area proportion was 79 percent.[40]

This overview of the changes in economic conditions affecting the production of wheat (also of rice) throughout many low income countries is based on the research of highly competent agricultural scientists. The distribution within and among countries of the high-yielding varieties then takes place. The necessary complementary agricultural inputs are produced and supplied. It is a highly complex process. A large array of economic disequilibria occur as a consequence of these changes during the process. Moreover, they continue to occur. Plant breeders keep on improving the high-yielding varieties. The natural environment counters with insects, various pests, harmful soil organisms and plant diseases. Prices of inputs and of wheat (rice) change. Economic disequilibria are pervasive. Moreover, additional disequilibria occur year after year.

Earlier we considered the motivations of wheat farmers in India. We argued that their motivation was to restore an equilibrium in their own economic domain. It was not to restore the equilibrium of the wheat economy of India. This argument is fully applicable to the responses of farmers throughout the low income countries included in Dalrymple's studies.

Lastly, there is as yet no evidence that the world wheat or rice economy, during the foreseeable future, will arrive at a stationary economic equilibrium. Nor is there evidence that wheat and rice yields will increase during the foreseeable future as much as they have since the mid-sixties. A long view of economic modernization is not that simple.

Notes and References

1 Gary S. Becker, "A Theory of the Allocation of Time," *Economic Journal*, 75, September 1965, 493–517.

2 R. H. Coase, "The Nature of the Firm," *Economica, N.S.*, 1, November 1937, 388.

3 W. David Hopper, "Distortions of Agricultural Development Resulting from Government Prohibitions," in *Distortions of Agricultural Incentives*, edited by Theodore W. Schultz, Indiana University Press, Bloomington, IN, 1978.

4 Zvi Griliches, "Hybrid Corn: An Exploration in the Economics of Technological Change," *Econometrica*, 25, October 1957, 501–22.

5 Ibid., p. 502, figure 1.

6 Ibid., p. 522.

7 Ibid., p. 519. See also Zvi Griliches, "Research Costs and Social Returns: Hybrid Corn and Related Innovations," *Journal of Political Economy*, 66, October 1958, 419–31; and

"Hybrid Corn and Economic Innovations," *Science*, 132, July 29, 1960, 275–80.

8 Don Paarlberg, *Towards a Well-Fed World*, Iowa State University Press, Ames, IA, 1988, ch. 11, pp. 79–86.

9 G. S. Tolley, "Management Entry into U.S. Agriculture," *American Journal of Agricultural Economics*, 52, November 1970, 475–93. This study provides strong support for an on-going selective process in a market economy.

10 Gary S. Becker, *Economic Theory*, Knopf, New York, 1971, ch. 7, p. 113.

11 Ibid., p. 125.

12 Zvi Griliches and William M. Mason, "Education, Income and Ability," *Journal of Political Economy, Part II*, 80, 1972, 74–103, on their "doubts on the asserted role of genetic forces in the determination of income."

13 Becker, *Economic Theory*, p. 123.

14 John Hicks, *Capital and Growth*, Oxford University Press, Oxford, 1965, ch. 3.

15 D. P. Chandhri, "Education and Agricultural Productivity in India," Ph.D. Dissertation, University of Delhi, 1968.

16 Finis Welch, "Education in Production," *Journal of Political Economy*, 78, January–February 1970, 35–59.

17 Zvi Griliches, "The Sources of Measured Productivity Growth: United States Agriculture, 1940–1960," *Journal of Political Economy*, 71, 1963, 331–46; and "Research Expenditures, Education, and the Aggregate Agriculture Production Function," *American Economic Review*, 54, 1964, 961–74.

18 Robert Evenson, "The Contribution of Agricultural Research and Extension to Agricultural Production," Ph.D. Dissertation, University of Chicago, 1968.

19 Research expenditures per farm were $4.30 in 1940 and $28.40 in 1959. The implication of Welch's analysis is that if research were to fall from $28.40 to $4.30 per farm about one-third of the differential would disappear. In my view, if there were no new agriculture research results for a decade, the technology of US agriculture would arrive at an economic equilibrium and the complexity of agricultural production would not require greater skills than those resulting from a high school education.

20 Wallace E. Huffman, "Contributions of Education and Extension in Differential Rates of Change," Ph.D. Dissertation, University of Chicago, 1972; "Decision Making: The Role of Education," *American Journal of Agricultural Economics*, 56, 1974, 85–97; and "Allocative Efficiency: The Role of Human Capital," *Quarterly Journal of Economics*, 91, 1977, 59–77.

21 It is noteworthy that the decline in price of nitrogen fertilizer was a consequence of a major technological advance. The development of the "Kellogg" process reduced sharply the real costs of producing nitrogen.

22 Todd Petzel, "Education and the Dynamics of Supply," Ph.D. Dissertation, University of Chicago, 1976.

23 Finis Welch, "The Role of Investment in Human Capital in Agriculture," in *Distortions of Agricultural Incentives*, edited by Theodore W. Schultz, Indiana University Press, Bloomington, IN, 1978, pp. 273–4 for a fuller account of Petzel's contribution. Other studies on education and allocative ability are reviewed by Welch in his 1978 essay and in my "The Value of the Ability to Deal with Disequilibria," *Journal of Economic Literature*, 13, September 1975, 827–46.

24 Marlaine E. Lockheed, Dean T. Jamison, and Lawrence J. Lau, "Farmers Education and Farm Efficiency. A Survey," *Economic Development and Cultural Change*, 29 (1), October 1980, 37–76.

25 Ibid., p. 61.

26 Dean T. Jamison and Lawrence J. Lau, *Farmer Education and Farm Efficiency*, Johns Hopkins University Press, Baltimore, MD, 1982, ix and 292 pages.

27 Thomas C. Cochrane, "Entrepreneurship," in *International Encyclopedia of the Social Sciences*, edited by D. T. Sills, Macmillan and the Free Press, New York, 1968, vol. 5, pp. 87–91.

28 Sherwin Rosen, "Authority, Control, and Distributions of Earnings," *Bell Journal of Economics*, 13 (2), 1982, 311–23.

29 Sherwin Rosen, "Specialization and Human Capital," *Journal of Labor Economics*, 1 (1), 1983, 43–9.

30 I am indebted to Robert E. Lucas, Jr, for this insight and example of the diversity of a person's abilities.

31 Reuven Brenner, *History – The Human Gamble*, University of

Chicago Press, Chicago, IL, 1984. Brenner deals extensively with discrimination and anti-semitism.

32 Welch, "The Role of Investment," pp. 259–81.

33 Rati Ram and Theodore W. Schultz, "Life Span, Health, Savings and Productivity," *Economic Development and Cultural Change*, 27, 1979, 399–421.

34 Dana G. Dalrymple, *Development and Spread of High-Yielding Wheat Varieties in Developing Countries*, Bureau of Science and Technology, Agency for International Development, Washington, DC, 1986, xi and 99 pages. A first edition was published 1969; all told six editions appeared prior to the 1986 referred to here.

35 CIMMYT is the acronym for International Maize and Wheat Improvement Center, Mexico.

36 Dalrymple, *Development and Spread of High-Yielding Wheat Varieties*, p. 18, table 2.2.

37 Ibid., pp. 34–5.

38 Ibid., p. 37, table 3.4.

39 Ibid., p. 85, table 4.3.

40 Ibid., p. 87, table 4.6.

10

Identifying Entrepreneurs by Transitory Income

Entrepreneurs do not carry identity cards, they publish no directory, they are nameless in the flood of economic statistics. Take a survey and ask, "Are you an entrepreneur?" The reply will be, "How do I know?" Observe what the person does and the question is, what behavior would be proof that he is an entrepreneur? Is the role attributed to an entrepreneur by Knight or by Schumpeter, von Mises, Coase or Kirzner observable?

A search for entrepreneurs would be in vain in an economy which is in equilibrium and in which all activities were routine and repetitive.

In looking for entrepreneurs, there are two reasons for not searching for them where the changes in economic conditions are very small. The smaller the change is, the less likely that entrepreneurship is observable. Thus, the distinction between small and not so small changes in economic conditions is important when it comes to identifying entrepreneurs. Whereas in principle both small and large changes require resource reallocations, when changes are very small the reallocations tend to be unobservable. When the price of poultry products declines slightly relative to that of beef nothing is gained by calling the observable substitution an entrepreneurial act. The same is true for the response of consumers to a small change in personal income or for the response of farmers to a small change in the price of fertilizer relative to other input prices.

In analyzing the economic value of schooling, the distinction between the work effect and the allocative effect of schooling on the production of self-employed economic agents has proven to be useful in identifying farm entrepreneurs, as is evident from Finis Welch's[1] research. We have drawn on his studies at some length. Entrepreneurial activity is readily observable when a large change in the price of an important input or output occurs, as was the case when oil prices more than doubled.

There is merit in the argument that the transitory income component provides a clue in identifying families that are entrepreneurial entities. We turn to it.

1   Transitory Income Approach

It is instructive to divide the personal income of families and individuals into two parts, namely, that which is perceived by the recipient to be transitory, and that which is viewed as permanent. Entrepreneurs, including entrepreneurial families who are engaged in restoring equilibrium in their economic domain, acquire a component of income that they perceive to be transitory income. They can be identified empirically by their relatively large transitory income component which is revealed in the changes in the assets and liabilities of the families. For farm families there is a substantial body of evidence which shows that they allocate relatively more of their income to purposes other than current consumption than nonfarm families who derive their income from wages and salaries. It is often said that many farm families live as if they were poor and die rich.

Milton Friedman[2] guided by his permanent income hypothesis found that the transitory income component of entrepreneurial families tends to be relatively large. It should be noted that in doing the empirical analysis he held that, "The precise line to be drawn between permanent and transitory components is best left to be determined by the data themselves...."[3]

Dorothy Brady and Margaret Reid let the data decide. So did Milton Friedman in testing his theory. Friedman[4] concludes his monograph by noting that over the period covered by his study, "... the ratio of permanent consumption to permanent income has been decidedly higher for wage earners than for entrepreneurial groups; from .90 to .95 for wage earners, from .80 to .90 for entrepreneurs...." *This difference between entrepreneurial and nonentrepreneurial groups in the size of this ratio seems larger and better established than any other that he has examined.* It does not come as a surprise that Brady, Reid, and Friedman *identified* farm families as entrepreneurial families. What is rare is their strong commitment to establishing the data to measure the transitory components of farm family incomes "... that show up primarily in changes of the consumer unit's assets and liabilities...."[5]

The Consumer Purchases Study reports are an important source of data concerning incomes of families, their expenditures for living, and the changes in their assets and liabilities during a 12 month period within 1935 and 1936 in small cities and villages and on farms. These studies were conducted under the auspices of the Work Projects Administration. The particular studies most relevant to the issue at hand are by Dorothy Brady[6] and her associates in the then Bureau of Home Economics of the US Department of Agriculture. It is unusual that the primary data on which empirical studies are based are published as fully as they are in these reports.

The large differences in the "transitory component" in the income of the families covered by the Consumer Purchases Study and also those in other studies were investigated by Margaret Reid.[7] Milton Friedman, in *A Theory of the Consumption Function*, drew in part on Brady's and Reid's findings in his empirical analysis. His results bear importantly on identifying entrepreneurs by the relative size of the transitory components.

An increase or decrease in the stock of family wealth provides a clue to the transitory income component. In the *Changes in Assets and Liabilities of Families,*[8] the part of family income not allocated to consumption is treated as a "net surplus." Where consumption exceeds family income a decline in wealth occurs, which is reported as a "net deficit."[9]

2 Data Limitations

Various limitations of these data are emphasized repeatedly by Brady, Reid, and Friedman. There are measurement errors in the reported changes in the value of assets and liabilities and in the estimated value of nonmoney farm income. The satisfactions that farmers derive from being self-employed producers are omitted. Data on the differences in age, schooling, and health of the members of the families, differences in the size of families, differences in real prices, in interest rates, and in risk both insurable and noninsurable are in large measure lacking.

The asset and liability status of farmers differs importantly by age. The ratio of debts to owned assets of young beginning farmers is as a rule high; at middle ages their assets tend to exceed their debts, and as they approach retirement they are at the stage in their life cycle when they become concerned about inheritance taxes. Although Margaret Reid is renowned for her analytical work on the economic effects of age, the data are not adequate to determine the age effects of members of farm families. The serious income consequences of the extraordinary drought in the Plains States and the governmental farm program effects are difficult to deal with.

Over the long term farmers find various ways of coping with adverse transitory income effects, in addition to holding nonhuman wealth to deal with income emergencies. To reduce the effects of expected adverse income events the available options are evaluated by farmers to a fine degree on whether such options are worthwhile.

For this purpose many farm families take advantage of part-time off-farm work by either the husband or wife, or by both, and by children who have reached the age to take on off-farm jobs. Other options to reduce the variance of their income include crop and livestock diversification, carry-over of feed grain stocks to maintain livestock when bad crops occur, the practice of fallow (where a part of the crop land is not cropped so that it can accumulate soil moisture which assures a better crop in the following year in locations where the fluctuation in annual rainfall is a critical factor in crop yields), and the practice of no-till-farming to reduce the losses of soil moisture. Nor do these options exhaust the possibilities. The effects of these options on measured farm family income and on the nature of the investments and current operating expenditures are in large measure not revealed by the data under consideration. The economic aspects of an array of actual types of investments that are made by farm families to reduce the variance in their income are considered in the next chapter.

Analytically the distribution of the transitory income variance within these sets of families and the limitation of using averages (although less so when using median incomes) are technical difficulties.

Despite these limitations a casual inspection of tables 10.1 and 10.2 reveals several telling clues pertaining to the entrepreneurial issue. The variance in total income of most sets of families is much larger than the variance in income allocated to consumptions! Corresponding to the behavior of families who derive their income from wages and salaries, the sets of farm families who derive their income primarily from dairying also devote a larger share of their income to consumption than do most other farm families. The wealth surplus component, indicated for the Michigan–Wisconsin

Table 10.1 Farm family income, consumption, and surplus or deficit, 1935–1936 (nonrelief families, including husband and wife native born)

| Location | Average income farm family | | Average value of consumption ($) | Average surplus ($) | or | net deficit (percentage of income) |
	Total income ($)	Money income ($)				
VT	1,177	732	1,156	26	(−5)[a]	2.2
NJ	1,553	1,022	1,567	−11	(−3)	−0.7
PA–OH	1,577	1,011	1,278	296	(+3)	18.8
MI–WI	1,325	864	1,247	85	(−7)	6.4
IL–IA	1,446	947	1,233	219	(−6)	15.1
KS–ND	823	400	1,181	−351	(−7)	−42.6
CO–MT–SD	1,069	686	1,149	−68	(−12)	−6.4
WA–OR	1,435	1,009	1,170	260	(+5)	18.1
OR, part-time	1,654	1,249	1,484	181	(−11)	10.9
CA	1,820	1,493	1,618	221	(−19)	12.1
NC–SC, white	1,546	947	1,340	208	(−2)	13.5
NC–SC, Negro	742	403	697	44	(+1)	5.9
GA–MS, white	1,418	943	1,130	281	(+7)	19.8
GA–MS, Negro	625	334	574	48	(+3)	7.7

[a] The figures in parentheses are the average balancing difference in dollars.
Source: Consumer Purchases Study, *Family Income and Expenditures, Farm Series*, Misc. Publ. 465, US Department of Agriculture, 1941, pp. 136–43, table 33.

Table 10.2 Family income and surplus or deficit, villages and small cities, 1935–1936 (nonrelief families that include husband and wife native born)

	Average family income ($)	Average net surplus or deficit (percentage of income)
Villages		
New England	1,537	0.8
Middle Atlantic and North Central	1,381	5.3
Plains and Mountain	1,497	4.9
Pacific	1,565	5.0
SE, white	1,674	7.7
SE, Negro	500	−0.4
Small cities		
North Central	1,734	10.3
Plains and Mountain	1,786	3.6
Pacific	1,954	6.6
SE, white	1,683	5.2
SE, Negro	620	0.6

Source: Consumer Purchases Study, *Family Income and Expenditures, Farm Series*, Misc. Publ. 464, US Department of Agriculture, 1941, p. 88, table 22.

set, is relatively small. The entrepreneurial function in dairy farming is less important than it is in most other types of farming. In the wheat farming sets of Kansas–North Dakota and Colorado–Montana–South Dakota, a considerable part of the consumption of farm families was made possible by reducing assets when coping with the adverse income effects of the severe drought. A comparison of the Washington–Oregon full-time farm families with the Oregon part-time set in table 10.1 indicates that the income variance of farm families who devoted a part of their time doing off-farm work was much less than the variance of those farm families who were full-time farmers.

The value of consumption of the two sets of Negro farm families is far below that of the other 12 sets. A decidedly high transitory income component is indicated for the Negro farm families based on the median income test reported in table 10.3. It is the preferred test.

Table 10.3 Indications of transitory income differences based on median income of farm families, 1935–1936 Consumer Purchases Study

Location	Net money income ($)	Expenditure for family living ($)	Minimum transitory ($)	Transitory as percentage of income ($)
VT	550	510	40	7.3
NJ	705	670	35	5
PA–OH	610	515	95	15.6
MI–WI	625	580	45	7.2
IL–IA	605	510	95	15.7
KS–ND	280	515	−235	−84
CO–MT–SD	470	580	−110	−23.4
WA–OR	680	550	130	19.1
OR, part-time	1,040	910	130	12.5
CA	1,070	1,040	30	2.8
NC–SC, white	550	500	50	9.1
NC–SC, Negro	345	285	60	17.4
GA–MS, white	360	340	20	5.6
GA–MS, Negro	230	190	40	17.4

Source: Margaret G. Reid, "Effect of Income Concept upon Expenditure Curves of Farm Families," in *Studies in Income and Wealth*, National Bureau of Economic Research, New York, 1952, vol. 15, p. 136, table 2.

Families in villages and in small cities during the 1935–6 period, on the evidence in table 10.2, were dealing with relatively small transitory incomes. Compared with the hectic economic circumstances of farm families, the economic life of families in villages and in small cities was serenely placid.

In view of the technical limitations of using average incomes, Margaret Reid selected the median income for analyzing the income–expenditure relationship "where the effect of transitory income was at a minimum." Based on the 1935–6 Consumer Purchases Study for farm families (units) she interpreted the results as conclusive evidence that families at the median income had far from a stable transitory income pattern. Reid's minimum transitory components for farm families by location are shown in table 10.3.

The last column in table 10.3 gives the minimum transitory component as a percentage of income. For the South the positive transitory component of the white farm families is much less than that shown for them in table 10.1. As noted above, the transitory income components for the two sets of Negro families based on their median income is decidedly higher than that shown in table 10.2. For the dairy farming sets, the Plains States wheat producers, and the Oregon part-time and full-time farm families, the median income results are similar to those appearing in table 10.1.

3   An Interpretation: Farm Families, 1935–1936

What was the relationship between the permanent income that these farm families expected and the income that they realized? Had they earned their income in villages or small cities in the same region, their reported family income would have been a closer approximation of their expected permanent income. In fact, urban wage and salary families reveal a small transitory income component.

Important as it is to have the 1935–6 data, they provide very little information on the economic circumstances and disequilibria that prevailed at the same time these families planned their income-producing activity and consumption for the 1935–6 period. There is a good deal of information from other sources that is relevant in determining what was expected.

The recovery from the Great Depression was still in process. The economic shock of 1932 was much more severe for the producers of grains and cotton than for dairy farmers.[10] Economic events during 1933 and 1934 gave rise to more favorable expectations. Compared with 1932, grain and cotton prices had more than doubled. Dairy product prices were comparatively steady, having risen only 14 percent. Government payments to farmers started in 1933. They increased sharply in 1934 when cotton, corn, wheat and tobacco producers received $605 million of such payments. Under the Agricultural Adjustment Act, the acres of these crops that were "retired" exceeded 35 million.[11] The 1934 government payments to hog producers were $200 million.

Farmers were quite aware of the fact that the very low farm product prices of 1932 were badly distorted relative to each other. They were also aware that the 1934 price relationships, except for the low price of meat animals, were close to normal, although farm prices in general were a third less than they had been in 1929. Many of the farm families in table 10.1 had not received and did not expect to receive government payments in 1935–6. It was known that payments to hog producers would be discontinued and that the cotton, wheat, and corn payments would continue into 1935–6. Farm families, as of 1935–6, did not include government payments in their expected permanent income.

The severity of the 1933 and 1934 droughts, predominantly in the Plains States where most of US wheat is produced, was unexpected. The droughts were dramatized by vast dust storms. Most of the data in table 10.1 for two sets of farm families where wheat is important were obtained in 1935 when only half of the winter wheat acreage seeded in the autumn of 1934 in Kansas, Colorado, and South Dakota was harvested. The average wheat production for 1928–32 in Kansas, Colorado, Montana, and North and South Dakota was 379 million bushels, whereas in 1934 it was a third as much, that is, 119 million bushels. The droughts also reduced corn yields sharply in those Plains States where some corn is grown. The 1934 corn yields in the western parts of the corn belt declined about one-fourth in Illinois and over two-fifths in Iowa and Minnesota.[12]

Lastly, farm families expected the mechanization of agriculture to continue. Tractors, trucks, and automobiles were replacing horses and mules. Combines, mechanical cornpickers, and milking machines were on the increase. The adoption of hybrid corn was just beginning.[13]

In view of the disequilibria that prevailed at the time these farm families planned their 1935–6 production and consumption, our interpretation of the reported changes in assets and liabilities is as follows. Farmers who specialized in dairying were affected least by the disequilibria consequences of the Great Depression, along with the consequence of government payments, droughts, and the rate of technological changes. Thus, Vermont and Michigan–Wisconsin families in dairy farming were relatively close to their then expected permanent income. For them the transitory income component was relatively small, and the implied entrepreneurial role was also small.

In the Illinois–Iowa set, where farmers specialized in producing hogs and corn, hog prices as of 1934 had not recovered as much from the 1932 Depression low as corn had recovered. Farmers expected hog prices to recover and the corn–hog price ratio to become more nearly normal, as it did. The government payments were viewed as transitory. They expected an increase in income from hogs despite the lower corn yields caused by the drought in 1934, which was in part offset by the increase in corn prices and the technological changes that were increasing production capacity. The implied net effect is that the expected positive transitory income component was large and entrepreneurial earnings provided a strong incentive to reduce the then prevailing disequilibria in their domain.

The large government cotton payments, in addition to the recovery of cotton prices, lend support to the interpretation that the reported incomes for white farm families in the four Southern states were somewhat on the high side. The transitory income components were moderate and positive. Here, too, entrepreneurial earnings were moderate. In sharp contrast, based on table 10.3, the Negro farm families were in a very low income state. They received virtually none of the government cotton payments. The productive capacity of the farms they operated was very small. My interpretation is that their transitory income component was large and their permanent income was very small.

Notwithstanding large government payments to wheat farmers and despite the recovery of wheat prices, farm family incomes in the Kansas–North Dakota wheat area were very low. Although assets were reduced, consumption was nevertheless low. The Colorado–Montana–South Dakota farm family set had much in common with that of Kansas–North Dakota. In interpreting the data of these two sets of farm families, one must consider the economics of droughts in the Plains States. Droughts and crop failures are expected. So are above normal rainfall years and bumper crops. The severity of the droughts during the mid-thirties could not have been anticipated. By means of self-insurance, some of the transitory income effects of the highly unstable crop yields on consumption were reduced. The rewards for entrepreneurial ability in farming in the Plains States are higher than in most of the other types of agriculture. In the Oregon part-time farm families set, nonfarm wages reduce the transitory income component. These farm families are in an economic domain which is comparable with that of city families. In the next chapter we shall examine the marked reduction in the transitory income component of farm families in the United States that has occurred as a consequence of the fact that over half of the farm families income is presently derived from off-farm sources.

4 A Summary

Entrepreneurs can be identified by their transitory income. The changes in assets and liabilities of urban, village, and farm families during 1935–6 made it possible to establish this identification. Dorothy Brady saw the transitory income components in her data. Margaret Reid extended Brady's analysis and also examined additional sets of data. Milton Friedman[14] proceeded to establish a strong linkage between entrepreneurship and transitory income. The entrepreneurial source of income of farm families and of owners of nonfarm unincorporated businesses makes the transitory components a relatively important source of the variations in their income. In Friedman's[15] words, ". . . entrepreneurial families, whether farm or nonfarm, are alike in being subject to much uncertainty with respect to their income; the standard deviation of their transitory components of income appears to be something over 40 percent of their mean income, or something like $1\frac{1}{2}$ to 2 times as large as for other families."

He[16] notes that, "The Dispersion of the transitory components is of the same order of magnitude for farm and nonfarm entrepreneurs. . . ." His view, however, that "nonfarm entrepreneurs apparently save a decidedly larger fraction of their income on the average" than farm entrepreneurs is subject to doubt, given the wealth that farm families tend to accumulate despite their relatively low average income.

Friedman's[17] generalization about consumer behavior based on the permanent income hypotheses stands repeating, namely that, ". . . the ratio of permanent consumption to permanent income has been decidedly higher for wage earners than for entrepreneurial groups . . . ," and that "The difference between entrepreneurial and nonentrepreneurial groups in the size of (this ratio) seems larger and better established than any other we have examined."

Notes and References

1 Finis Welch, "Education in Production," *Journal of Political Economy*, 78, January–February 1970, 35–59.

2 Milton Friedman, *A Theory of the Consumption Function*, Princeton University Press, Princeton, NJ, 1957.

3 Ibid., p. 23.

4 Ibid., p. 227.

5 Ibid., p. 221.

6 Dorothy S. Brady (senior author), Consumer Purchases Study, Urban, Village and Farm, *Changes in Assets and Liabilities of Families, Five Regions*, Misc. Publ. 464, US Department of Agriculture, 1941, 226 pages. Also, *Family Income and Expenditures, Five Regions, Farm Series*, Misc. Publ. 465, 1941, 366 pages.

7 Margaret G. Reid, "Effect of Income Concept upon Expenditure Curves of Farm Families," in *Studies in Income and Wealth*, National Bureau of Economic Research, New York, 1952, pp. 133–74, and "The Relations of Within-Group Transitory Component of Incomes to the Income Elasticity of Family Expenditures," Unpublished Paper.

8 Brady, Consumer Purchases Study, Misc. Publ. 464 and 465.

9 The specific wealth components that are identified in the changes in assets and liabilities are reported in detail.

10 The price farmers received for grains and cotton in 1932 were about one-third of what they had been in 1929 prices. Dairy product prices, however, in 1932 were at 53 percent of 1929 prices (US Department of Agriculture, *Agricultural Statistics*, 1937, p. 400, table 498).

11 Ibid., pp. 414–15, table 513.

12 *USDA Yearbook of Agriculture*, 1935, p. 380, table 43.

13 Zvi Griliches, "Hybrid Corn and the Economics of Innovation," *Science*, 132 (3422), July 29, 1960, 275–80; also, "Hybrid Corn: An Exploration in the Economics of Technolo-

gical Change," *Econometrica*, 25 (4), October 1957, 501–22.

14   In Friedman, *A Theory of the Consumption Function*, chapter on "Occupational Characteristic of Families," p. 69. Two of the rare qualities of this book are: (a) the preface in which the "unrivaled knowledge of the empirical evidence from family budget data" of Dorothy Brady is generously acknowledged. Then follows the "characteristic enthusiasm, persistence, and ingenuity" of Margaret Reid in her endeavor to put the permanent income hypothesis to a critical test.... "This book is the result, and though my hand held the pen, she pressed me to write up the underlying theory..."; (b) as an advance in economic theory and in the application of that theory in empirical analysis, the quality of this book is rare indeed.

15   Ibid., p. 77.

16   Ibid., p. 78.

17   Ibid., p. 227.

11

Micro Behavior in Reducing Income Variance

How do families and individuals deal with variances in their income? Measured income and measured consumption reveal an important part of their behavior that is motivated by these variances. There is another part of their behavior, however, that antedates measured income and consumption. It consists of actions that were taken by them to reduce the expected variance in their income. The main purpose of this chapter is to consider economic events and conditions that motivate families and individuals to reduce the variance in their income.

One of the implications of the permanent income hypothesis[1] is that the variance in measured consumption is less than the variance in measured income. Strong evidence is presented in support of this implication in the preceding chapter. But the observable income and consumption variances do not reveal to what extent and by what means families and individuals had reduced these variances. The possibilities and the incentive to reduce them are important in understanding this micro behavior. A good deal is known about the possibilities of reducing the variance in assets and liabilities.

But much less is known about the economics of various means that families and individuals use to reduce the expected variance in their income. When there are possibilities that make it worthwhile to reduce the expected variance in income, the implication is that economic agents perceive that they are in a state of disequilibrium and that they stand to gain from restoring an equilibrium in their micro domain.

Farm families have been dealing with income variances for ages. Most farms have a long history. Most farm families know much of the history that is specific to the economic properties and location of their farm. They have discovered ways of reducing particular income variances at costs that made it worthwhile. The economist, however, is rarely privy to this private history and to the true income expectations of entrepreneurial farm families.

The difference in the effects of expected and unexpected variances in income is useful. But if the variance in income is a function of *true uncertainty*, there is no action that an economic agent could have taken that would have altered the income variance that occurs as a consequence of a true uncertainty event. The resulting unexpected profits or losses from such events, however, have income effects that induce the economic agent to revise his planned income and also his planned consumption. In this chapter we shall not pursue the economic implications of true uncertainty profits and losses, although they occur frequently and are important in the observable rise and fall of families.

In dealing with expected variance in income, families and individuals search for information and draw on their experience to evaluate the sources of the variation in their income. They know that the "natural" variance in their income would be greater than the measured variance had they not taken actions to reduce the "natural" variance.

We proceed guided by the proposition that when the cost of reducing the income variance is less than the value that the family or individual agent expects to derive from the reduction, there is an incentive to act. The existence of such an opportunity implies that there is an economic disequilibrium that it is perceived, and that the incentive is sufficient to take action to reduce the income variance. The human agent who perceives and acts, given these circumstances, is an entrepreneur.

Restoring an economic equilibrium when there are incentives to reduce income variances entails entrepreneurial acts that go beyond the standard concept of "allocating resources." The incentives may be sufficient to bring about institutional changes in property rights and changes in the legal bases of cooperatives, of cash and share leases, of credit arrangements, and of legal rules pertaining to bankruptcy. Institutional changes pertaining to the functions of the family are also important. A later chapter deals with changes in the family under changing economic conditions.

Incentives to restore equilibrium and by what means these are exemplified are noted in each of the following economic circumstances.

1   By Means of Farm Plots

In many locations over a long span of English history tillers of the soil produced their crops typically on many small plots that were widely scattered. They spent much time in going from plot to plot as they did their field work. From the viewpoints of land reformers and historians, it was hard to imagine a more inefficient system of allocating land by location for the purpose of producing food. It was deemed to be proof that this type of traditional farming was wasteful, inefficient, and irrational. This history of scattered farm plots presented a puzzle for economists for it implies that these particular economic agents, whether they are labeled cultivators, peasants, or farmers, were not calculating human beings who equated marginal costs and returns.

Donald McCloskey[2] found the solution to this puzzle. As is true of many discoveries, what McCloskey discovered turned out to be surprisingly simple and compellingly valid. He began with the fact that, "In much of England, from the earliest times to the nineteenth century, peasants held their

land in many little scattered plots ... some 20 acres in the
fields of his village in twenty or so separate locations."
McCloskey proceeds to prove that this situation, in terms of
costs and returns, was an economic maximization in allocating land resources by locations. The underlying economics of
scattered plots turns out *not* to support the "common sense"
views of the proponents of the enclosure movement and those
of historians who argued that scattered plots were a highly
inefficient use of farm land. McCloskey states their case
against scattered plots succinctly. They saw it as "... a most
peculiar way to hold land, or at any rate so it has seemed to
most observers of the system since the first enthusiasm for
enclosure in the sixteenth century, because it appears to
reduce output, a strange burden for a community near
starvation to assume. The most obvious loss is the time spent
wandering from plot to plot . . ."[3]

The key to the economics of scattered plots prior to the
agricultural revolution, under the technical possibilities including variations in weather and in soils and the economic
circumstances, was that scattered plots reduced the annual
variations in food production. Scattered plots reduced the
probabilities of a crop failure; scattered plots made it possible
to produce enough food in most bad crop years to avert
famine. McCloskey's solution of this long-standing puzzle of
the scattered plots is a neat contribution in economics.

2   Reducing Yield Variance by Summer Fallow

Wheat yields in semi-arid areas are decidedly vulnerable in
low rainfall years. The variability of annual rainfall in these
areas is as a rule large. Tilling cropland without sowing it for
a season is to fallow the land. In the spring wheat areas it is
referred to as *summer fallow*. The area of summer fallow as a
percentage of the area sown to crops in the Prairie Provinces
of Canada and the adjacent states of the United States
increased sharply after 1910. In Saskatchewan the use of

summer fallow, as a percentage of grain crops sown on fallowed land, increased from 12 to 66 percent between 1911 and 1960.[4]

Ross Parish's[5] analysis of the economics of summer fallow in spring wheat is a comprehensive empirical test of three hypotheses in explaining the increased use of fallow. The first hypothesis is that fallowing occurs as a response to changes in the relative prices of the factors of production. He found substantial support for this hypothesis based on the decline in land prices relative to that of other farm input prices. Summer fallow was a means of substituting land for other inputs. The second hypothesis is that fallow occurred as a response to the declining productivity of land. He found little support for this hypothesis. The third hypothesis is that farmers turned to fallow to reduce the yield variance caused by drought throughout the spring wheat area. In these particular arid areas, fallowing did reduce the variance in wheat yields caused by below normal rainfall in areas especially vulnerable to droughts.

The entrepreneurial ability of these wheat farmers in dealing with large reductions in yields caused by below normal rainfall is exemplified in part by the shift to summer fallow and then to less tillage to reduce the loss of soil moisture.

3   Changing Leases to Deal with Income Variance

Farm tenants beware: when the economy is expected to continue in an unsettled state, choose a crop share lease; when the economy is performing at steady pace and is expected to continue to do so, choose a cash lease.

Observable shifts from cash to crop share leases and then back to more cash leases as economic conditions have changed lend support for these choices. The tenure effects of large changes in the level of farm income and in the variance of that income on choice of farm leases are exemplified by what occurred in Iowa between 1927 and 1939.[6] This study leaves enforcement and supervision costs aside. Clearly, at the outset of this period where farming was prosperous and farm income was relatively stable, there was a shift to cash leases. By 1930, cash leases had increased to 45 percent of all leases. Then, in response to the unstable economic conditions that occurred after 1930, cash leases declined to a low point of 18 percent of all leases by 1934. At that juncture conditions began to improve, and by 1939 cash leases accounted for 45 percent of all leases as they had in 1930.[7] The changes in economic stability during the 12 year period had decidedly strong effects on shifts between types of farm leases.

During the unstable economic conditions of the early thirties, farm families who rented the land they farmed under a crop share lease were less vulnerable to the variance in their incomes than those who farmed under a cash lease.

In the thirties, most farms in the Corn Belt were operated either by tenants or by owners who were not free of debt. Farmers who had title to part of the land that they farmed and who leased additional farm land were classified as part-owners. They were numerically a small group. Another small group consisted of owners who were free of mortgage debt. They accounted for only 19 percent of all farms in Iowa in 1930.

The implied conditions were as follows: (a) a substantial proportion of farm families did not have sufficient assets of their own to operate and to own their farms; (b) those with insufficient assets sought to supplement their own resources by obtaining additional resources either by renting land or by borrowing funds; and (c) both creditors and landlords in supplying capital to these farmers imposed constraints in varying degrees which had marked effects on costs and returns of farmers. Farmers who borrowed capital to acquire ownership of farms in general operated farms that were smaller than the farms of those farmers who rented the farms they operated. The set least vulnerable to the large variance in income owned their farms free of debt, but their farms were a good deal smaller than the tenant operated farms.[8]

A study by C. H. Hanumantha Rao[9] of changes in farm tenure in India during the fifties, before the new high-yielding varieties of wheat and rice became widely available, provides additional evidence on farm income variance and farm tenure. Both the scope of entrepreneurship and the variance of the farmer's income differ significantly between cash rents that are agreed to in advance of production and rents fixed in kind, also agreed to in advance of production, and sharecropping rental agreements. Most of the empirical part of Rao's study is based on West Godavari (Andhra) data, a rice area.[10]

Rao found that lease arrangements are influenced by the relative importance of the entrepreneurial function. In India sharecropping tends to prevail in areas where there is little scope for decision making pertaining to product, as well as to factor substitution, and where the rewards for entrepreneurship are low. Fixed cash rent tends to increase where entrepreneurial earnings are significant. The evidence does not indicate measurable inefficiencies in the use of land under sharecropping. As new cropping opportunities occur, however, entrepreneurship becomes more important.

According to Rao,[11] "The incentives for sharecropping arrangements may persist as long as the benefits from reducing the variance of income outweigh the possible benefits from the use of the available modern inputs...."

4   Effects of Off-Farm Employment on Choice of Farm Lease

Off-farm employment earnings reduce the income variance of farmers. The purpose of Richard Dowell's[12] analysis was to determine the effects of off-farm earnings on a farmer's tenure choice. His hypothesis implied that the effect would be a preference for cash leases. His evidence and analysis strongly support this hypothesis. His study shows that as more off-farm job opportunities become available the demand for less risky forms of farm tenure shifts to the left, implying that the demand for share rent contracts decreases relative to that for cash rent. His tests are based on US data by states, and on Mississippi and Illinois data by counties. "In seventy-one of the seventy-five regressions, covering the period from 1890 to 1970, the relation came out significantly positive!"[13]

Dowell[14] also measures the effects of farm income variances on choice of tenure and the effects of type of farming on choice of tenure. His findings are that the locations with the higher yield variance have more tenancy than those with relatively less variance. The effect on choice of tenure, using data at the county level based on the *1960 Census of Agriculture*, strongly supports the implied hypothesis.[15] Dowell[16] also tests for the effects of mean wealth, wealth distribution, and scale of farming on tenure choice. The scale argument is supported. The wealth argument is not supported; although the estimates have the right signs, they are not significant: "... cross-sectional variations in mean income between counties are positively correlated with off-farm employment in bad crop years and negatively correlated in good crop years relative to wealth."[17]

Most of Dowell's research was devoted to the effects of off-farm employment opportunities on tenure choice. His results based on the period from 1890 to 1970 strongly support the implications of his hypothesis, namely that off-farm employment increases the demand for cash leases.

5   *In Planning for Emergencies*

The uses of resources to deal with emergencies that are expected are revealed in observable changes in family assets and liabilities. The allocation of human capital is also a part of planning for emergencies. But evidence on the role that human capital plays in dealing with emergencies is hard to come by and theoretical thinking has not been especially helpful.

In Friedman's[18] view, presented in his treatment of "Motives for Holding Wealth," human wealth is not suited for emergencies. His argument is that a major general distinction exists between human and nonhuman wealth. Human wealth is deemed to be unsatisfactory when, "a reserve is needed for protection against an *unexpected occurrence* threatening the realization of a planned level of consumption...."[19] Two points are at issue here.

1 If a future emergency were truly unexpected, it would be unknowable to the family when it makes its consumption plans. It would be a true uncertainty emergency. Thus, whether it be nonhuman capital or human capital to provide a source of income with which to cope during an expected emergency, the family, be it an entrepreneurial family or not, must have some comprehension of the probabilities of the occurrence of the emergency. Accordingly, however dim the perceived probabilities, the emergencies that matter in this context are not truly unforeseeable.

2 People who act as economic agents in making plans to deal with expected emergencies are not restricted to using non-human assets for this purpose. Their human capital, which consists of their abilities revealed in the value of their time, are also used in making plans for this purpose.

The British knew, to quote Morris David Morris,[20] that their "Indian Budget was a gamble on the monsoon." During the 76 years from 1875 to 1950, 152 floods and 124 droughts in various parts of India were recorded. One bad crop is not a test of the ability of farm people to survive. Morris analyzes an array of survival devices that these people developed and used. The variability of the monsoons is recognized by areas. The "agriculturists calculate the costs of survival not for a single year but for the length of what local experience suggests is a full weather cycle."[21] One device consists of a reciprocal arrangement between farmers who live in different areas to transfer cattle from an area that lacks feed and water[22] to an area that has been spared the specific drought. Another well-known survival device is to accumulate, during good crop years, a reserve of gold and silver ornaments worn by women.

What is less well known are (a) reciprocal arrangements for some members of a farm family from a drought stricken area to migrate and live with a family in an area that is not in a state of emergency; (b) income derived from wages is diversified by having some of the adult members of extended farm families enter upon work in another area to provide a steady source of wage income for the extended farm family that strive to survive a serious extended period of droughts (floods); and (c) seasonal precautionary migration of some members of a farm family occurs regularly to increase "the ability of a whole family to better survive adverse periods."[23]

In their 1981–2 study of education in rural South India, John C. Caldwell et al.[24] note that this "population is deeply conscious of the pattern of periodic drought-induced disaster, and an important security strategy has been to seek, for some of the family, local off-farm employment or full-time urban occupations." The argument is that the better the education of the family members the more useful this strategy is in reducing the toll from periodic famine.[25]

Kenneth Wolpin's[26] analysis of the effects of weather on income and consumption of farm households in India based on 2061 observations over three crop years, 1968–9 to 1970–1, shows surprisingly small income and consumption effects, although 48 percent of these households experienced some adverse weather in 1968–9 compared with less than 17 percent of the same households in 1970–1.[27] The following data are adjusted for price inflation. They show that farm income per farm in 1968–9, when 48 percent of the village

representatives reported some adverse weather, was 10 percent below that of 1970–1, the best year. Income per family
from all sources in 1968–9, however, was only 2 percent
below that in 1970–1. Consumption including expenditures
on durables showed virtually no change (table 11.1).

Table 11.1 Self-reported income and consumption per family
in rupees

	1968–9	1970–1[a]	1968–9/ 1970–1
Adverse weather (% of farms)	48	17	2.82
Farm income (per farm)	3,283	3,666	0.90
Income from all sources (per family)	4,329	4,422	0.98
Consumption including durables (per family)	3,271	3,292	0.99

[a] The rupee estimates for 1970–1 are adjusted for 9.4 percent inflation
during this period.

The poorest agricultural families in India are predominantly landless. Their nonhuman assets are minimal. They derive
virtually all their income from work. They know that there
will be emergencies. Past experience over generations tells
them the dire state to expect. Their options for dealing with
such expected emergencies are dismal at best. Their income in
kind and in wages from work leaves these families very
vulnerable.

A preliminary survey of what these various experiences in
reducing income variances have in common shows that the
family perceives that a disequilibrium exists and that it is
worthwhile to restore an equilibrium. By doing so the family
reduces the variance of its income and this action identifies it
as an entrepreneurial family. What it does entails entrepreneurship, be it by means of scattered farm plots, summer
fallow, off-farm employment or shifts in leases. These are

some of the ways of reducing particular income variance in farming. So, too, were the responses of US farm families to the highly unstable economic events associated with the 1935–6 period, as is evident in the Brady, Reid, and Friedman studies.[28] Most farm families in their studies were endeavoring to restore an equilibrium in their private economic domain.

6   *Reducing Income Variance of Farm Families in an Unstable Economy*

Increases in real income is an identifying attribute of a progressive economy. The resulting increases in income of many families occur unevenly. In such an economy agriculture is subject to particular micro income disequilibria which are consequences of a syndrome of changes that originate in various parts of the economy. These changes account for most of the unstable income of farm families. As the variance of the income derived from farming increases, what are the options of farm families to improve their economic circumstances?

Where migration from farms to cities is permissible, many farm families leave agriculture. Where planning is long term, children of farm families become oriented and prepared in terms of their human capital, mainly schooling, to earn their income in nonfarm sectors. Where a marriage market serves both farm and nonfarm youth, farm-reared females, more so than males, opt for a marriage that takes them out of agriculture. There is a search by farm families for sources of income that are more rewarding, for sources of income that have less variance, and for locations where they can maintain a farm residence and obtain off-farm employment.

Aspects of the economic importance of off-farm income have been considered in this and the preceding chapter. Data are now available for a comprehensive view of the economics of off-farm income in a large national economy. Beginning

with 1960, the US government has published annual estimates of the income that farm families derive from off-farm
sources. Off-farm income does not include government payments to farmers. The economic setting and scope of the
changes during this period require some elaboration.

Changes in US agriculture during recent decades have been
many and large, large enough to be readily observable.
Family and hired labor employed in agriculture declined from
10.5 million in 1929 to 5.5 million in 1960 when off-farm
income estimates were first reported. By 1986 only 3.2
million were thus employed.

As of 1935, there were 6.8 million farms, by 1960 slightly
less than 4 million, and by 1986 only 2.2 million. Total farm
output, however, doubled between 1934 and 1960 and then
increased another 50 percent by the mid-eighties.

Movements of people out of US agriculture have not
occurred at a steady rate. Nor have they been blissful. They
have not been neutral in their effects on the variance of the
income of those who left and of those who remained in
agriculture. The rate at which these movements of people will
occur is not knowable. Families and individuals, whether they
are rural or urban, are likely to be perplexed by the many
different changes in economic conditions. Nor can policy
makers or economists anticipate, as of any given date, the full
array of economic changes under way and the resulting
disequilibria that would entail movements of people.

After the fact it is clear that these movements out of
agriculture are far from steady. At times they take a reverse
turn. As evidence, consider the net movement of people into
US agriculture that occurred during 1932 and 1933. The
movement out of agriculture again reversed itself in 1946.
Annual net movements of people out of US agriculture ranged
from less than a half to eight-tenths of a million during
1936–40. In 1943 it was well over 3 million. From 1948 to
1970 there were nine scattered years when the net annual
out-movement ranged from 1 million to 2.2 million. On this

migration issue, beware of the assumption that it occurs at some steady rate. Likewise, the changes in physical and human capital and changes in technology are such that steady state economics is not applicable.

A preliminary inspection of table 11.2 suggests that the variance in farm family income derived from farming is much larger than that from off-farm sources, especially when account is taken of the difference in the trends of these two sources and when the much enhanced income instability of the eighties is examined. As the income instability of these families increases, they seek sources of income that reduce the variance in their income by increasing their reliance on off-farm earnings. Several of the means of making such shifts were analyzed at the outset of this chapter. In US agriculture, increases in off-farm income relative to that derived from farming has become an important means in stabilizing farm family income. Table 11.2 estimates do not indicate the rates of changes in off-farm income prior to 1960, but the table does show that already as of that date 42 percent of farm family income came from off-farm sources (table 11.2, column 6). Beginning with 1965 and through 1979, except for 1973 when the income from farming increased greatly, the share of off-farm income ranged from 50 to 57 percent of the total.

During the first eight years of the eighties, off-farm family income increased markedly relative to that from farming. It was also a period of extraordinary income instability from farming which ranged between 4,480 and 13,830 in nominal dollars per farm family (table 11.3, column 6).

Two additional perspectives based on income changes expressed in 1967 dollars are as follows:

1   The 1986 net farm income per family was $4,211, only a fourth larger than it had been in 1960, whereas the off-farm income component was $6,117 in 1986 compared with $2,413 in 1960, a two and a half fold increase.

Table 11.2 Number of farms and per farm operator net farm income and per farm off-farm income, 1960, 1965, and 1970–1986

1	2	3	4	5	6
Year	Number of farms (thousands)	Net farm income per farm family ($)	Off-farm income[a] per farm family ($)	Total income per farm family ($)	Off-farm income as percentage of total income per family (%)
1960	3,960	2,910	2,140	5,050	42
1965	3,360	3,840	3,790	7,630	50
1970	2,950	4,880	6,000	10,880	55
1971	2,900	5,180	6,590	11,770	56
1972	2,860	6,820	7,440	14,260	52
1973	2,820	12,200	8,760	20,960	42
1974	2,800	9,780	10,070	19,850	51
1975	2,520	10,140	9,480	19,620	48
1976	2,500	8,060	10,690	18,750	57
1977	2,460	8,070	10,640	18,710	57
1978	2,440	11,350	12,190	23,540	52
1979	2,430	13,300	14,510	27,810	52
1980	2,430	4,480R	14,260	18,740	76
1981R	2,430	8,420R	14,700	23,120	63
1982R	2,400	6,750R	15,160	21,910	69
1983R	2,370	3,040R	15,600	18,640	84
1984R	2,330	11,560R	16,450	28,010	59
1985R	2,285	11,250R	18,600	29,850	62
1986P	2,240	13,840P	20,090	33,930	59

It is assumed that there is one operator family per farm. Updated through 1986.

R, Revised Economic Indicators of the Farm Sector, *National Financial Summary*, 1986, p. 48, table 37; P, preliminary.

[a] Off-farm income includes income from off-farm activities such as wages and salaries, nonfarm businesses, interest, dividends, rents, and transfer payments. Off-farm wages and salaries account for about three-fourths of the reported off-farm income.

Source: US Department of Agriculture, Economics Research Service, *Economic Indicators of the Farm Sector, Income and Balance Sheet Statistics, 1983*, Washington, DC, 1984, p. 74, table 50.

Table 11.3 Purchasing power in 1967 dollars of the per farm family off-farm income and net farm income, 1980–1986

1	2	3	4	5	6	7	8	9
						Purchasing power (1967$)		
Year	Number of farms (thousands)	Total off-farm income ($ billion)	Off-farm income per farm ($) (3 ÷ 2)	Total net farm income ($ billion)	Net farm income per family ($) (5 ÷ 2)	Off-farm income per family income ($) (4 ÷ 9)	Net farm income per family income ($) (6 ÷ 9)	Consumer price index, all items (1967=100)
1980	2,428	34.7	14,260	10.9	4,480	5,778	1,816	246.8
1981	2,434	35.8	14,710	20.5	8,420	5,399	3,092	272.4
1982	2,401	36.4R	15,160	16.3R	6,750	5,227	2,335	289.1
1983	2,370	37.0R	15,600	7.2R	3,040	5,395	1,018	298.4
1984	2,328	38.3R	16,450	26.9R	11,560	5,290	3,715	311.1
1985	2,285	42.5R	18,600	25.7R	11,250	5,776	3,493	322.2
1986	2,240P	45.0P	20,090	31.0P	13,840	6,117	4,211	328.4

Source: US Department of Agriculture, Economics Research Service, *Economic Indicators of the Farm Sector*, National Financial Summary, Washington, DC, 1985, p. 12, table 1; update based on USDA *Agricultural Outlook*, August 1987, table 32.

2 The standard deviation of the 1980–6 family income from farming at its mean was three times as large as that of the income derived from off-farm sources.

The evidence we have examined supports the proposition that farm families shift to more off-farm income when their income from farming becomes more unstable. For US agriculture in its entirety, as of 1960, 42 percent of the income of farm families came from off-farm sources. This component of their income increased relatively and substantially during the seventies and then during the 1980–6 period when their income from farming became highly unstable; off-farm income accounted on average for 67 percent of the total farm family income.

The above evidence, however, conceals important differences among farms and farm families. The US Department of Agriculture official definition of a farm is that it has annual farm product sales of $1,000 or more. A typical classification of farms by *sales classes* is shown in table 11.4.

Each of over a third of all farms in 1983 had less than $5,000 of sales. The net loss of those in this sales class from farming was $687 per farm. Presumably the residence of the families in this sales class was in the countryside where they produced a few farm products that were sold, and in general one or more members of the family commuted and worked for a wage or a salary. The off-farm income of this set of families in 1983 was $21,090 per family. Is it meaningful to treat this large subset of families as farm families? Farmers they are not.

Except for their residence and their home produced food, most of these families had completed their movement out of agriculture. The economic kinship between this class and the next two sales classes is close. Although the $5,000–$9,900 and the $10,000–$19,900 sales classes had a fragile link to agriculture by virtue of larger sales which, however, entailed larger losses, these two classes had slightly less off-farm

Table 11.4 Per farm sources of income by sales classes, 1983

1	2	3	4	5	6	7
	Farms			Per farm income sources		
Sales class ($ thousand)	(thousands)	(%)	Net farm income ($)	Off-farm income ($)	Total ($) (4 + 5)	Off-farm as percentage of total (%)
Less than 5	829	35.0	−687	21,090	20,403	103
5– 9.9	325	13.7	−812	20,050	19,238	104
10– 19.9	279	11.8	−1,053	18,060	17,007	106
20– 39.9	272	11.5	303	13,547	13,850	98
40– 99.9	381	16.1	4,800	11,253	16,050	70
100–199.9	177	7.5	14,050	11,790	25,840	46
200–499.9	83	3.5	35,400	14,610	50,010	29
500 and over	24	1.0	416,200	28,600	444,800	6.4
All farms	2,370	100.0	6,794	17,300	24,094	72

Table 11.3 revisions were not made in this table.

Source: US Department of Agriculture, Economic Research Service, *Economic Indicators of the Farm Sector, Income and Balance Sheet Statistics, 1983,* Washington, DC, 1984, tables 60, 68, and 69.

income and less total per farm family income. These three sales classes accounted for 60 percent of all farms (farm families) based on the official definition of a farm.

A part of the evidence appearing in table 11.4 reveals a great deal about the process of the movement of people out of agriculture. The less than $5,000 sales class has virtually completed this moving process. Sales classes $5,000–$9,900 and the next higher set were far along in doing so. Even the $20,000–$39,900 sales class, as of 1983, received little net income from farming.

The variance of the economic value that families derive from the food they produce for home consumption and from the rental value of their dwelling is very low. Both of these income components, however, in effect reduce the total income variance. Their relative economic importance is highest for the smallest sales class and lowest for the top sales class. There has been a marked decline in food that farm families produce for their home consumption, whereas the importance of the dwelling component has been increasing decidedly.

For the sales class with the largest sales, the income stabilizing effect of the off-farm income component is small by virtue of the fact that it accounted for only 6.4 percent of the total income per farm of this class (table 11.4). For this sales class, nonmoney farm income imputed to farm produced food for home consumption is a very small source of income. In absolute amount the imputed rental value of dwellings is large relative to other sales classes but it, along with the food item, is an exceedingly small source of income of families in the highest sales class.

Income and consumption data for 1935–6, a legacy of the research led by Dorothy Brady, provide information for various types of farming with detailed estimates of changes in assets and liabilities. Comparable data for more recent dates are not available. The 1980 survey by the National Opinion Research Center provides farm income estimates for 1979.

Table 11.5 US per farm off-farm earnings of men and women and net farm income by regions, 1979

	1	2	3	4	5	6
	Off-farm earnings				Total per farm income (3 + 4)	Off-farm earnings as percentage of total
	Men	Women	(1 + 2)	Net farm income		
New England	10,690	3,360	14,050	10,360	24,410	58
Mid Atlantic	6,520	1,680	8,200	22,000	30,200	27
E–N Central	8,860	2,680	11,540	14,950	26,490	44
W–N Central	6,230	3,310	9,540	17,500	27,040	35
South Atlantic	9,630	2,960	12,590	10,500	23,090	55
E–S Central	9,730	3,060	12,790	10,210	23,000	56
W–S Central	10,450	3,120	13,570	10,700	24,270	56
Mountain	7,230	3,150	10,380	14,900	25,280	41
Pacific	13,670	5,090	18,760	12,370	31,130	60

The figures in columns 1–5 are average dollars per farm.
Source: Based on Table 5 in William Sander, "Off-Farm Employment and Income of Farmers," Oxford Agrarian Studies, 1983, 34–47.

These estimates are available by regions, but not by types of farming areas. Table 11.5 is from William Sander's study. It shows off-farm earnings of men and women separately. In other respects it supplements and supports earlier parts of this chapter.

7 Summary

In the short term a greater stability of consumption is achieved mainly by changes in assets and liabilities, and by having recourse to human capital earnings of family members. Over the long term economic agents have the entrepreneurial ability to search, discover, and devise worthwhile ways of reducing the variance of the income on which they are dependent. Measured income does not reveal the extent to which the observed income variance has been reduced.

Any truly unforeseeable increase or decrease in income is a function of true uncertainty. Whatever is unknowable cannot be anticipated. When events occur that are in the domain of true uncertainty, the resulting unexpected profits or losses have income effects that induce economic agents to revise their planned income and planned consumption.

Studies of various means to reduce the variance in income over the long term were examined. Tillers of the soil in early England learned that scattering the land they farmed into small plots reduced the year to year variations in food production and they thereby averted most crop failures and their starvation consequences. The practice of summer fallow in parts of Canada and the United States reduces crop failures in low rainfall years and thus reduces the income variance of farmers producing wheat in such areas. Farmers who rent some or all of the land they farm reduce the income variance from farming by shifting between cash and crop share leases. The choice of farm lease is also affected by the opportunities for off-farm employment. Off-farm employment increases the demand by farmers for cash leases.

In planning for emergencies, too little attention is given to the economic importance of human capital. A reserve to protect the planned level of consumption against serious declines in farm products and income over a span of two or even more years is not restricted to holding physical wealth. The use of human capital for this purpose is being documented for farm families in India.

Income diversification that complements production specialization has been occurring through much of US agriculture. On-farm specialization may make farm families more vulnerable to the variance in their income from farming. Off-farm income reduces this variance. It has become an increasing share of total farm family income. For all farm families this component of their annual income in recent years has accounted for well over half of the total income. The evidence is strong in support of the proposition that off-farm income reduces the income variance of farm families, and the larger the share of farm family income from off-farm sources the smaller the total income variances.

Notes and References

1 Milton Friedman, *A Theory of the Consumption Function*, Princeton University Press, Princeton, NJ, 1957, p. 222.
2 Donald N. McCloskey, "English Open Fields as Behavior Towards Risk," in *Research in Economic History: An Annual Compilation of Research*, edited by Paul Unselding, JAI Press, Greenwich, CN, 1976, vol. 1, pp. 144–70; also his "The Persistence of English Common Fields," in *European Peasants and Their Markets: Essays in Agrarian History*, edited by W. N. Parker and E. L. Jones, Princeton University Press, Princeton, NJ, 1975.
3 Ibid., p. 124.
4 As of 1960, about half as much land has been under fallow in the United States as has been seeded to wheat and so, too, in the Prairie Provinces.
5 Ross M. Parish, "The Economic Significance of Summer Fal-

lowing in the Spring-Wheat Regions of North America," Ph.D. Dissertation, University of Chicago, December 1972. The data in the above paragraph are from tables 1 and 2 of Parish's dissertation. See also E. Lloyd Barber, "Summer Fallowing to Meet Weather Risks in Wheat Farming," *Agricultural Economics Research*, 3 (4), October 1951, 118–23; Dale A. Knight, "Economic Considerations for Selecting the Superior Frequency of Fallow for Wheat in Three Locations in Western Kansas," Kansas Agricultural Experiment Station, Technical Bulletin 85, September 1956.

6 Theodore W. Schultz, "Capital Rationing, Uncertainty, and Farm-Tenancy Reform," *Journal of Political Economy*, June 1940, 309–24. The main part of that paper dealt with the constraints on borrowing capital to own and operate a farm compared with the owned assets that are required when farms are rented from the owners of farms.

7 Ibid., pp. 320–1.

8 Ibid., p. 316, table 2.

9 C. H. Hanumantha Rao, "Uncertainty, Entrepreneurship, and Sharecropping in India," *Journal of Political Economy*, 79, May–June 1971, 578–95.

10 Ibid. Rice and tobacco lease contracts are analyzed; incentives for factor substitutions are the heart of this study; some references are made to Ludhiana (Punjab), a wheat area (pp. 583–92).

11 Ibid., p. 593. The effects of the differences between cash and share leases on supervision and enforcement costs are considered by Rao.

12 Richard Samuel Dowell, III, "Risk Diversification and Land Tenure in United States Agriculture, 1890 to 1970," Ph.D. Dissertation, University of Chicago, August 1977.

13 Ibid., p. 50. Dowell's data are presented on pages 65–72, tables 1–5, for "cash tenants" over "share tenants," "owners" over "tenants," "full owners" over "part owners," and "owner plus cash" over "share tenants."

14 Ibid., pp. 51–3. Data on page 80, table 8.

15 Ibid., pp. 53–4 and pp. 86–90, tables 10 and 11.

16 Ibid., p. 54.

17 Ibid., p. 57.

18   Milton Friedman, *A Theory of the Consumption Function*, Princeton University Press, Princeton, NJ, 1957, pp. 16–17.
19   Ibid., p. 16, emphasis added.
20   Morris David Morris, "What is a Famine?" *Economic and Political Weekly*, 44, November 2, 1974, 1855–64.
21   Ibid., p. 1856.
22   Comparable with what some drought-ridden farmers in South Dakota did in the mid-thirties when they shipped their work horses to Virginia where they were fed and cared for until the horses were returned for spring work.
23   Ibid., p. 1957.
24   John C. Caldwell, P. H. Reddy, and Pat Caldwell, "Educational Transition in Rural South India," *Population and Development Review*, March 1985, 29–51.
25   Ibid., p. 29.
26   Kenneth I. Wolpin, "A New Test of the Permanent Income Hypothesis: The Impact of Weather on the Income and Consumption of Farm Households in India," *International Economic Review*, 23 (3), October 1982, 583–94.
27   Ibid., p. 589, table 1.
28   Presented in considerable detail in chapter 10.

12

Entrepreneurial Components in Research

Organized research is a difficult activity to foster, promote, and finance in ways that will optimize the creativity of individual researchers. Research that is undertaken to create new resources or to increase the productivity of existing resources has become an important specialized sector in many modernizing high income economies. The high rate of increase of this sector during recent decades implies that it is deemed to be a worthwhile activity.

Marshall[1] stressed the importance of knowledge in production, to wit, "Knowledge is the most powerful engine in production; it enables us to subdue Nature and force her to satisfy our wants." Contrary to the now fashionable view, Nature is neither benevolent nor bountiful when it comes to food. To produce the food to satisfy human wants entails the cultivation of much harsh land subject to the vicissitudes of weather and climate. Marshall perceived what every farmer and agricultural scientist knows, namely, the niggardliness of raw land and the hostility of pests, insects, and soil organisms to agricultural production. A major task of research oriented institutions is to create "knowledge" that will increase the ability of man, for the purpose at hand, to produce food. Funds, scientists, and organizations are necessary but not sufficient. What is also required in creating knowledge is a specialized component consisting of *research entre-preneurship*. It is a scarce ability; in research it is hard to identify this talent; it is rewarded haphazardly in the not-for-profit research sector, and it is impaired by over-organization.

To create a high-yielding food crop requires highly specialized human capital, consisting of geneticists, biologists, plant breeders, and other specialized scientists. It also requires an organized institutional arrangement and funds, and an entrepreneurial component. The state of what is known in economics about the creation and distribution of new resources and about new ways of increasing the productivity of existing resources is still fragmentary.

1   Lost Historical Perspective

Why history? Although most people still cherish their roots, most scientists do not waste their time on history. Nor do economists as they become more "scientific." Hayek's[2] dictum stands repeating: "Nobody can be a great economist who is only an economist," and he added, "an economist who is only an economist is likely to become a nuisance if not a positive danger." It is fully as true for scientists in this age of minute specialization. Avoid history, discover a small bit of new knowledge, and you have the makings of another crisis. Without history, current events produce much pessimism. He who is an optimist is either isolated or committed to the belief that there is a thread of historical continuity in the human condition, and that it is not altogether bad.

Andre and Jean Mayer[3] have stated imaginatively an important aspect of the history and utility of the sciences in agriculture.

> Few scientists think of agriculture as the chief, or the model science. Many, indeed, do not consider it a science at all. Yet it was the first science – the mother of all sciences; it remains the science which makes human life possible; and it may well be that, before the century is over, the success or failure of Science as a whole will be judged by the success or failure of agriculture.

There is much criticism of agricultural and food research that is a part of the Land Grant institutions in the United States. What is lost sight of is the gradual evolution that has characterized these institutions since the Civil War. They started without prestige, with few students who were qualified for college work, and there were few scientists to be had in recruiting a faculty. They faced antagonists and harassment of competitors, yet they managed to survive and they have become robust, tough, and successful. It would be surprising if they had no weaknesses. In general the weaknesses are not those that most critics belabor.

The public funds that support agricultural research in these institutions come increasingly from the respective states. Thus the state-supported part of this research is not under the centralized control of the federal government, which is one of the strong features of US organized, publicly supported agricultural research. I shall argue that it would be a mistake to eliminate this freedom of research decisions of the respective states.

The benefits from close association of agricultural research workers with other scientists have increased over time; thus the comparative advantage of on-going agricultural research that is associated with a major research oriented university is strong and clear.

There has been enough history to measure the returns from agricultural research. Given time the benefits are transferred largely to consumers. During the early decades of the Land Grant development the research contributions were small; this inference is supported by the first studies of Vernon Ruttan concentrating on agricultural productivity. But after the late twenties the productivity effects of agricultural research became important. We now have competent studies by Zvi Griliches on hybrid corn and sorghum, Willis Petersen on poultry, Robert Evenson and Yoav Kislev on US agriculture in general, and others – all treating agricultural research as an investment. The rates of return have been high compared with normal alternative investment opportunities.

We also learn from these studies that it may take many years before returns are realized, as it did in the case of hybrid corn. A theory of hybridization dates back to 1905. Public research expenditures began in 1910. They continued year after year. The first returns became evident after 1933. As of 1955, the accumulated past research expenditures on hybrid corn came to $63 million. By then the annual returns had become very large.[4]

We can ill afford to lose sight of the successes of private and public organized research in the case of agriculture and food. But to see this accomplishment requires a historical perspective. Without it, it is all too easy to become frustrated and depressed by the facile doomsday stories, limits of growth, and all manner of predicted food crises. In the face of these, little wonder that there is much pessimism. The niggardliness and vicissitudes of Nature are not new. We are not about to control the weather. Although knowledge is a powerful engine in the production of food, nevertheless food always has been scarce, and it never will be a free good. Moreover the view that food can be made abundant everywhere in the world during a short period is not consistent with the time it has taken the United States with all her skills, resources, and organized research to modernize agriculture and make it highly productive.

2   *Entrepreneurship and Research Hypotheses*

There are two entrepreneurial functions in organized research. One of these entails assessing the frontier of the relevant sciences to determine the most promising hypotheses to be pursued. The other function is that of attaining an economic equilibrium in the allocation of the resources available for this research.

A convenient assumption is that a well organized research institution competently administered will perform both of these functions adequately. In fact, however, a large research organization that is tightly controlled is the death of creative research because no administrator of a large complex research organization, consisting of many research projects, can know the array of research options that the state of scientific knowledge and its frontiers afford. Nor can a manager of foundation funds know what needs to be known to perform this function. Most working scientists are entrepreneurs on the choice of hypotheses. But it is exceedingly difficult to devise institutions to utilize their entrepreneurial talent efficiently.

Organization is necessary. Agricultural research has benefited from its experiment stations, specialized laboratories, and from the recently developed international agricultural research centers. But there is the ever present danger of over-organization, of directing research from the top, of requiring working scientists to devote ever more time to preparing reports to "justify" the work they are doing, and to treat research as if it were a routine activity.

3   Neglect of Price Signals

The scarcity of agricultural resources – land relative to labor and both of these relative to the stock of reproducible forms of physical capital – is a major consideration in determining the types of research that are required for the economy of any country. The historical responses of agricultural research in various countries to these resource scarcity considerations are well established. The evidence on this process is presented by Hayami and Ruttan[5] in their well-known book on agricultural development.

There are three reasons for the neglect of price signals in organized research: (a) a belief exists that prices are too unstable to be useful signals; (b) a desire prevails to free organized research from any intrusion by special interest agents; and (c) the actual price signals to which the organized research might respond are frequently distorted prices for reasons of governmental policy.

Prices in this context include the economic value of the service of the land (rent), the services of reproducible forms of capital ("interest"), and the value of human time (wages, salaries, and entrepreneurial earnings). They are information signals and incentives to work and to invest which entail all manner of resource allocations, including the allocation of resources for research. Prices accordingly are indeed relevant. If there were no prices, we would have to invent them. Various countries have invented their internal prices. Their inventions, however, have worked badly in the case of agriculture. They have also had adverse effects on the agricultural research of these countries.

The desire to free research from particular types of intrusion has merit. The idea that research should produce knowledge that is deemed to be "appropriate" in accordance with the social values of some scientists, coupled with the intent of Congress that federally supported research should be applied, is a serious adverse intrusion.

Economic analysis distinguishes between the class of research that profit oriented firms can *do* to their advantage and the class of research where the benefits are too widely diffused to be captured by private firms. If we are to have the benefits of the class of research that firms do not undertake, we must have not-for-profit research. The latter class of research has been and no doubt will continue to be important.

With rare exceptions, farms are too small to do their own research, whereas many corporations in the nonfarm sector do much of their own. Some of the applied research being done in experimental stations could be done for profit by business firms that produce inputs and services for the agricultural sector.

In most countries price signals of the market are distorted by government policy. These price distortions are a serious economic problem throughout the world. In general, the price distortions not only reduce but often destroy the economic incentives of farmers to adopt the results of research that would increase the productivity of agriculture. I first examined this problem in "Uneven Prospects for Gains from Agricultural Research Related to Economic Policy."[6] In 1977, I organized a three day workshop on Distortions of Agricultural Incentives.[7] This class of distortions continues to burden agricultural and food sectors.

4 International Agricultural Research Centers

Policy issues pertaining to the International Agricultural Research Centers provide some additional information about the basic problems presented at the outset of this chapter.[8]

Some over-organization is evident

The research success of the International Agricultural Research Centers is not in doubt. It is the allocation of the available funds to the Centers and to the agricultural scientists who do the actual research that results in some identifiable efficiency losses. Those who control the purse strings cannot know what the involved agricultural scientist knows. Nor can they comprehend the vast heterogeneity of agriculture.

This issue also burdens agricultural research in the United States. A 1982 report on *Science for Agriculture*[9] is in essence a plea for more centralized control of this research in the United States. The fatal flaw of that report is its failure to comprehend the specific nature of research that is oriented to the requirements of agriculture. Agricultural production is soil specific, crop and plant variety specific, animal production specific, market specific and inescapably location specific. Because of all these specific characteristics, agriculture is by its very nature exceedingly heterogeneous. Even within most states, agriculture is far from homogeneous and so is the required research. To assume that a government agency in

Washington, blessed with a highly competent administrator who has at his service the best peer review, the best computer technology, and a highly competent staff could determine the optimum agricultural research that is required in the United States is wishful thinking. Priorities and control of agricultural research all vested in Washington would be a disaster akin to the agricultural failure of Gosplan.

As argued above, when an agricultural scientist is required to spend a lot of his valuable research time justifying his research, it is a signal that there is too much organization. Beware of organization that impairs the research creativity of the individual scientist.

Lack of funds for salaries in low income countries

This unsolved problem is specific to that large part of the world where wages, salaries, and per capita incomes are low.

Competent specialized agricultural scientists are a critical and an essential input in this research. They are scarce. The demand for this class of specialized skills has increased greatly. At salaries that prevail in most low income countries, qualified individuals are not to be had. The reason is clear. For an individual to become a competent agricultural scientist entails a large investment in a specialized form of human capital. Where the salaries for such skills are low, the supply that is required to do successful research will not be forthcoming. Within the confines of International Agricultural Research Centers, this salary issue is solvable by location. But it has not been solved in most of the national agricultural experiment stations and agricultural research laboratories throughout the low income parts of the world.

It would be selling economics short not to point out once again that *research entrepreneurship* is a critical factor in the performance of organized agricultural research.

5   *Failure to Reckon the Consumer Surplus Derived from Research*

We should keep on asking "Who benefits from agricultural research?" That which is done by private firms is done for profit. It is becoming increasingly evident as agricultural modernization proceeds throughout the world that an increasing share of agricultural research in open economies is being undertaken by private firms.

Appeals to farmers for public financial support are being thwarted by unsolved surplus problems in North America and Western Europe. Moreover, the concerned governments are finding surpluses ever more costly. In most low income countries, farmers have relatively little political influence whether it be for or against public funds for agricultural research.

There are several important unsettled empirical issues: Under what conditions and for how long a period do farmers benefit from particular research contributions? Some farmers acquire a short term "producer surplus" while other farmers producing the same product suffer a "producer loss"; the issue is "why?" How long does it take competition to transfer and transform the benefits from agricultural research into consumer surpluses?

Three decades ago I presented evidence that appropriations by states revealed strong urban support for agricultural research. Land grant institutions with large funds to support agricultural research of high quality are to be found, increasingly, in particular urban states.

The urban and labor political influence is also evident in the US Federal Food and Agriculture appropriation process which includes federal funds for agricultural research. Here, too, there is evidence that funds for agricultural research are not viewed by urban people as harmful. On the contrary, they appear to perceive that they benefit from such funding.

The marked decline in the costs of producing wheat and corn is well documented. Agricultural research accounts for much of it. So, too, has the cost of many other agricultural commodities declined, despite the strong secular increases in the value of human time devoted to farming in high income countries.

The reduction in the cost of food is an important factor accounting for the decline in the part of the consumers' income that is spent on food. Since poor families benefit relatively more from the decline in costs of food than families who are not so poor, there is an income effect; namely, what occurs is some reduction in the inequality in the distribution of real income.

We must see clearly the economic importance of the consumer surplus that results from successful agricultural research. The fact that agriculture is a declining sector of an economy does not imply that future consumer surpluses will not be forthcoming. The case for public financial support for agricultural research should be strongly linked to the achievable consumer surplus.

6   *Will Agricultural Research Grind to a Halt for Lack of Advances in the Sciences?*

In the event of an extended period during which no advances in the sciences were realized, investment in agricultural scientists and in the other inputs that are required for agricultural research would manifest strong diminishing returns.

Theoretical elaborations of economic models win high marks for subtlety, refinement, elegance, and for some of their analytical properties, but they do not tell us what is likely to happen in the sciences during the next 20–25 years. Judgments on what is happening and what is likely to occur, taking a long view, involve issues and reasoned arguments that call for long conversations. My argument would be that the rate of increase in the advances in the sciences has not as yet peaked. As feed stock for agricultural research, there will be additional advances to warrant more agricultural research.

The implication of my long view of the economic value of agricultural research is such that it calls for a continuation of increases in agricultural research to serve agricultural modernization and, in so doing, *create consumer surpluses.*

7 Agricultural Research and Growth Theory

Growth theory has lost its analytical charm. In explaining growth it has been found wanting. As noted repeatedly throughout this study, the treatment of technological advances as an exogenous variable takes much of the economics out of this source of income increases. By the early fifties, on seeing that the increases in agricultural outputs were exceeding the increases in agricultural inputs, this puzzle became a basic unsolved economic problem. One approach was to find the source of each observable technological advance and determine its cost and returns with the view of transforming it into an endogenous variable. Another approach that has been rewarding is to ascertain the increases in acquired human abilities as components of human capital.

Compared with the long history of agriculture, that of organized agricultural research is short. The high rate of increases of agricultural research during recent decades tells a good deal about the perceived value of this research. As of 1987, the population of the world had doubled since 1950, having passed the 5 billion statistic. World food production, however, had more than doubled since 1950, unevenly among nation-states to be sure. A clue to the demand for this research is in the more than sevenfold increase in real expenditures worldwide on agricultural research since 1950.

Malthusian population experts, vintage 1950, who were wedded to the Ricardian concept of land as the only source of food, proclaimed that there would soon be a world food crisis. On the contrary, a remarkable increase in agricultural food production was achieved by many low income countries. This achievement would not have been possible had there been no agricultural research.

8   Bare Bones of Research

To review: Public supported agricultural research is done in experimental stations, in research laboratories, and at centers that have acquired an international dimension. It requires specialized scientists. It also requires research entrepreneurs. These abilities are scarce and they account for most of the costs. The fact that agricultural research is institutionalized does not make it immune to changes that occur in the economic domain in which the research is situated. Research costs and the resulting research returns, covering recent decades, have received a good deal of analytical attention by economists.

However, the economics of agricultural research was still in its infancy as recently as 1950. Much has been learned since then. The costs of organized agricultural research, staffed with qualified scientists, are well documented in the case of public expenditures. But all too little is known about the international labor markets with particular reference to the factors that determine the salaries that are paid to highly competent scientists. Also lacking is information pertaining to international markets for modern scientific equipment. The nature and the significance of the imbalances between basic and applied research are for the most part still unknown, although there is much talk about such imbalances. The economic value of the research output is more difficult to ascertain than the public expenditures for it. How much to invest in this activity is a basic issue.

9 An Investment Approach

Treating research as an investment requires a long view. Valuable research results are not to be had like picking fruit in the wild. Hybrid corn is one of the great research success stories. As noted, it took over 20 years of research to develop a high-yielding variety of hybrid corn deemed to be ready to be used by farmers. The rate of return on this investment in research has been and continues to be higher than the prevailing "normal" rates of return.

To grasp the nature and economics of the research process, a short view will not do. Confined to a short view, one becomes beholden to highly inelastic supplies of agricultural products, whereas a long retrospect assessment reveals that supplies have increased more than demands have over time. Then, too, the Ricardian concept of agricultural land loses its economic stranglehold on agricultural production, as research discovers new ways of augmenting the capacity of land, ways that are in effect substitutes for land. The result is that the effective supply of such land does not remain fixed in quantity, in quality, or by location. The productivity of land is in large measure man-made.

10 Changes in Demand

What drives the demand for agricultural research? For that which is done by private firms, it is profitability. But profits from this specific research activity are not reported. What we know is that such research expenditures by industries that produce farm inputs to supply modernized agriculture are large. For the United States for 1979, we have an estimate from Vernon Ruttan[10] that amounts to between $814 and $909 million of expenditures on farm input research and, in addition, $270 million on farm machinery and equipment including that for farm transportation. The total purchases by

US farmers of fertilizer and other plant nutrients, pesticides, various other chemical and biological agents, fuels, petroleum products, equipment and machinery, and others totaled $71 billion in 1979, of which $19 billion were manufactured inputs.

The economic argument for public sector agricultural research rests on a strong body of evidence which shows that the benefits from this activity have been and continue to be large.

11   *Changes in Supply*

To review, agricultural research is a specialized activity that creates new agricultural resources. Successful agricultural research increases the supply of such resources. The economics of creating this knowledge takes us into the domain of human capital. It takes human capital to produce human capital. Over time human capital has become increasingly more specialized. Scientists are highly specialized human capital and it takes scientists to produce scientists. Moreover, specialization abounds. There are two critical limitational factors. They are (a) the supply of competent specialized agricultural scientists (plant breeders have held the spotlight during the recent past), and (b) the advances in the sciences.

The availability of land for experimental plots is a minor factor. Additional experiment stations and research laboratories can be had in a few years, provided there are funds to pay for construction. The required modern scientific equipment is somewhat harder to come by. The *critical input consists of competent specialized agricultural scientists.* They are scarce. At salaries that prevail in most low income countries, all too few are to be had.

While it takes much time, all the inputs that are required to increase the supply can be augmented. We know that some research results that prove to be valuable have taken decades to achieve.

A lack of advances in the sciences would be a potential limitational factor. In the event of an extended period during which no advances in the sciences were realized, investment in agricultural scientists and in the other inputs that are used in agricultural research would manifest strong diminishing returns.

12 Endogenous Increases in Productivity

The origins of increases in economic productivity are basic in identifying the sources of increases in income. They originate either from outside or from inside the economy. Schumpeter used this dichotomy effectively in his theory of economic development. It is applicable to various other sources of economic changes in addition to the contributions of innovators.

In searching for the origins of the components of economic productivity, one finds that virtually all these components are man-made and originate from inside the economy. Keep in mind that the sun, the earth, the winds, El Niño or La Niña[11] are not in the business of increasing our economic productivity.

In the case of wheat in India, we await a theory of economic productivity to rationalize this extraordinary event. We should try to explain why in the Punjab the rates of return to land, fertilizer, equipment, labor, and to the entrepreneurship of farmers all exceed normal rates for a period of years.

The economics of hybrid corn, including all the complementary inputs, the value of the output from the crop land released from corn, the reductions in the costs of feed to producing livestock products, and the resulting consumer surpluses all occur inside the economy. They are basic economic components in explaining the increases in income from economic modernization.

Here we have strong clues as to why farmland rents decline

as a fraction of national income and why the economic influence of landlords declines socially and politically.

13   Interpretations and Implications

Where there are advances in the sciences and where the economy is changing as it is being modernized, organized research requires entrepreneurship. This entrepreneurial component has two functions. One entails assessing the frontier of science to ascertain the most promising hypotheses to be pursued, and the other function is to restore an economic equilibrium in the allocation of the available research resources as economic conditions and research opportunities change.

The economics of restoring equilibrium, including that within organized research, is still in its infancy. The search for increasing returns got lost in the growth theory hubbub. The increasing returns insights of Marshall and also of Allyn Young are being rediscovered. Schumpeter's innovator is one of the human agents who increases economic productivity. What this innovator does is performed inside the economy. But does he create a disequilibrium or does he see that a disequilibrium exists and then proceed to profit from restoring equilibrium?

Investment in human capital matters greatly. The internal private effects of human capital are well documented. The economics of private and public investment in research and development is robust. What is known is being under-utilized in explaining the economics of increases in production, income, and welfare.

The rates of increase in investments in agricultural research worldwide are high. The high returns from this set of investments have propelled this expansion. There is some over-organization. The salaries of highly qualified agricultural scientists are too low in low income countries. The case for funding agricultural research should be based mainly on its contribution to consumer surpluses.

Notes and References

1 Alfred Marshall, *Principles of Economics*, 8th edn, Macmillan, London, Book IV, ch. 1, second paragraph.

2 F. A. Hayek, "The Dilemma of Specialization," in *The State of the Social Sciences*, edited by Leonard D. White, University of Chicago Press, Chicago, IL, 1956, pp. 462–73.

3 Andre and Jean Mayer, "Agriculture: The Island Empire," in *Science and Its Public: The Changing Relationship*, *Daedalus*, Summer 1974, 83–95. See also the excellent essay by Edward Shils, "Faith, Utility and the Legitimacy of Science," in the same issue of *Daedalus*.

4 See Zvi Griliches, "Research Costs and Social Returns: Hybrid Corn and Related Innovations," *Journal of Political Economy*, 66, October 1958, 419–31, tables 1 and 2. The $63 million accumulated past expenditure is based on ˉ 5 percent rate of interest. Using a 10 percent rate, these expenditures came to $131 million. The dollar figures in the text and in this note are in 1955 dollars.

5 Yujiro Hayami and Vernon W. Ruttan, *Agricultural Development: An International Perspective*, 1st edn, Johns Hopkins University Press, Baltimore, MD, 1971.

6 In *Resource Allocation and Productivity*, edited by Thomas M. Arndt, Dana G. Dalrymple, and Vernon W. Ruttan, University of Minnesota Press, Minneapolis, MN, 1977, pp. 578–89.

7 Theodore W. Schultz (ed.), *Distortions of Agricultural Incentives*, Indiana University Press, Bloomington, IN, 1978.

8 Here I draw in part on my "Value of Research, Endogenous Technology and Economic Progress: The Case of Agriculture," presented at Latin American Econometrics Society Meeting, August 2, 1988.

9 *Science for Agriculture* deals with issues in American agricultural research based on a workshop report held at Winrock, June 14–15, 1982, and published by The Rockefeller Foundation, New York, 1982, 35 pages.

10   Vernon W. Ruttan, *Agricultural Research Policy*, ch. 8, "The Private Sector in Agricultural Research," University of Minnesota Press, Minneapolis, MN, 1982.

11   Richard A. Kerr, "La Niña's Big Chill Replaces El Niño," in *Science*, August 26, 1988, 1037–8. Also in the same issue of *Science*, pp. 1043–52, by COHMAP members.

13

Institutions and Property Rights

A strong connection exists between investment in human capital and the secular rise in the economic value of human time. The institutional implications of this development are far from clear. What is evident, however, is that the rise in the value of human time makes additional demands on institutions. Some political and legal institutions are especially subject to these demands. Moreover, the process of restoring equilibrium as these changes in demand occur is an important analytical issue.[1]

Our approach is designed to explain those changes in institutions that occur in response to the process of economic modernization. An institution is treated as a supplier of a service which has an economic value. It is assumed that the process of growth alters the demand for the service and that this alteration in the demand brings about a disequilibrium between the demand and the supply measured in terms of changes in costs and returns. The supply of the services of an institution may be altered by factors other than economic growth.

It might be said that human capital is protesting the status quo of institutions as it seeks property rights for itself. We have enough historical perspective to see that the ownership of land is declining as a source of economic leverage, as is the ownership of physical capital relative to that of human capital. We have long known that Ricardian rent is not the real fulcrum of economic values, nor is physical capital the critical historical factor as early economists believed. The institutions governing property rights in land and in other forms of physical capital are far from adequate in providing property rights for human capital. Would that economics could have been blessed by the marriage of Irving Fisher's[2] all-inclusive concept of capital and John R. Commons'[3] *Legal Foundations of Capitalism.*

It has become a mark of sophistication in economic models not to mention institutions. It is significant that economists, despite this omission, manage somehow to find support for institutional changes, but it cannot hide the fact that, in thinking about institutions, too little attention has been given to this analytical part. There are a few old boxes labeled "institutional economics" which have been pushed aside and which have long been thought to be empty. When we look more closely we observe changes in institutions, but economic analyses of these economic functions are few. Yet it is evident that particular institutions really matter, that they are subject to change and are, in fact, changing, and that people are trying to clarify social choices with regard to alternative institutional arrangements to improve the economic efficiency and welfare performance of the economy.[4]

Since I deal only with those institutions that affect economic functions, I leave aside all institutions that perform other functions. It is my aim to consider particular political, including legal, institutions that in one way or another influence, or are in turn influenced by, economic modernization. It is a concept of institutions which is in the domain of political economy. A partial list includes institutions that reduce transaction costs (for example, money and markets), that influence the distribution of risk (contracts, share tenancy, cooperatives, corporations, insurance, public social security programs), that provide linkages between functional and personal income streams (property rights, inheritance laws, seniority and other rights of labor), and that establish the framework for the production and distribution of public goods and services (highways, airports, schools, agricultural experiment stations).[5]

For each of these services there is a demand. It is therefore within the province of economics to approach the determination of the economic value of each of these services by treating them in terms of supply and demand and placing each of such services into an equilibrium framework. The key assumption in taking this step is that people, as economizing agents, strive for an equilibrium with respect to each of these economic services of institutions.

It is all too convenient to assume that the economy produces additional income streams over a period of time in such a way that no disequilibria occur.

The process of economic modernization is beset by all manner of disequilibria. Institutions that perform economic functions are not spared. Some of these disequilibria persist and even become chronic. A long-standing disequilibrium has burdened human agents in agriculture. It persists despite the extraordinary migration out of agriculture. C. E. Bishop,[6] in his perceptive analysis, clearly identified the difficulties in altering community institutions. With respect to this and other disequilibria, the questions to be asked are: Can equilibrium be restored more efficiently than is the case presently? How can this be done? How can restoration be achieved at a cost where the benefits will exceed the cost?

1   *Institutions Serve and Constrain the Economy*

For economic analysis an institution is a special entity that has the attributes of a rule. The origin of such a rule is either social, political, or legal. Its origin is not beyond the reach of historical studies. Observable institutions are exemplified by the rules that govern marriage and divorce, rules embodied in constitutions that govern the allocation and use of political power, and rules that establish market oriented capitalism or governmental allocation of resources.

2   Search for Economic Effects of Legal Institutions

My first research assignment was given to me by John R. Commons. It was to search for the historical circumstances that gave rise to the legal negotiability of a debt. To promote the efficiency of trade fairs, the Common Law of England established a legal rule that made such debts negotiable instruments.

Contracts are a viable institution. They also undergo changes, for example in extensions of the capital market to provide funds to invest in one's human capital. The legal rights of labor become more important as the value of human time increases. Rules governing organized labor have both legal and political origins. So do the institutionalized rules that govern the centralization of government. There are many more such institutions in this set. They are a rich vein for search.

It is hard to believe that institutions such as these are immune to economic analysis. The analytical job is to specify their functions, measure their influence, and determine when they are efficient. To get on with this task requires a theory from which testable hypotheses can be derived. The hypotheses, we may hope, will lead to empirically valid propositions pertaining to the economics of institutional changes.

It will not do to omit these institutions, Nor will it do to impound them and thereby abstract from them. Nevertheless, that is the approach of the mainstream of economics. Economists with all their analytical tools are not analyzing the interactions between institutional changes and economic modernization.

One must give credit to those few hardy economists who

remain committed to institutional economics. In their concern about property rights in natural resources, they are best known for analyzing and arguing for land reform. The essence of their work is to begin with an *ad hoc* institutional change. It is therefore not an approach that treats an institution as an endogenous variable. It is primarily concerned with the effects of a particular reform upon the distribution of personal income and welfare.

I digress to consider briefly several testable propositions pertaining to institutions and agricultural production. Various testable hypotheses are pursued in my *Transforming Traditional Agriculture*.[7] When agriculture acquires a growth momentum as a consequence of new high-yielding food crops, the process of increasing production induces farmers to demand institutional changes. They demand new types of credit, with stress on timeliness, and they organize cooperatives for this purpose. They demand more flexibility in tenancy contracts. They join with neighbors to acquire tube wells and other investments to improve the supply of water. Both tenants and landowners use whatever political influence they have to induce the government to provide more and better large-scale irrigation and drainage facilities. These are all testable propositions. There is a growing body of evidence in support of each of these propositions.[8]

Thinking in terms of economic incentives that induce institutional responses which are a consequence of economic modernization, there are these additional general propositions.

1 In a market economy which is achieving increases in income, the demand for the convenience of money increases.

2 In an economy in which the income per family is rising, the demand for contracts and property arrangements serving families and consumers increases.

3 As economic modernization becomes increasingly dependent upon the advance in knowledge, the demand for institutions that produce and distribute such knowledge increases. In producing and distributing knowledge the less developed countries are in general substantially more in disequilibrium than are the technically advanced countries.[9]

4 When economic development reaches the stage at which the economy requires increasingly higher skills, the demand for skills that require schooling, including higher education, increases relative to the demand for low skills and for reproducible forms of nonhuman capital. (There is strong evidence that the US economy has been in this stage since the Second World War.)

5 In an economy where increases in the economic value of human time are being achieved, the demand for a number of different institutional services increases. As human lives become more valuable, the demand of workers for additional safeguards protecting them from accidents becomes stronger.[10] So does the demand for health services and for life insurance. The demand for additional legal protection of personal rights also increases, as does the demand more generally for civil rights. As a factor in production, human agents demand greater equality in obtaining jobs, especially so with respect to jobs that require high skills. Closely related is the increase in the demand for less discrimination in accessibility to schooling and higher education to acquire the higher skills. As consumers, human agents demand greater equality in having access to consumer goods and services, notably in housing and leisure activities. As the value of human time rises, institutional changes occur that favor good-intensive consumption activities.

3 Human Capital Property Rights

The remarkable secular rise in tl e economic value of human time that has occurred in the Un. ̇d States and in other high income countries is the source of major disequilibria in the economic functions performed by institutions. I argue that additional public provisions for legal services for the poor, programs to alleviate poverty,[11] and the Supreme Court's decisions with regard to schooling are institutional responses to increases in the value of human time. Although it might be maintained that these changes, including urbanization as an intermediate influence, are not dependent upon economic modernization's enhancing the economic value of human time, it is a weak argument. These institutional changes are predominantly consequences of the economic modernization that has been occurring. These legislative acts and legal decisions were, in large part, made possible and necessary because of the particular processes of achieving increases in income. In brief, these legislative and legal changes are accommodations to the institutional stresses and strains brought about by the marked secular rise in the economic value of human time.

It is hard to imagine any secular economic change that would have a more profound influence in altering institutions than would the movements in the value of wages relative to that of rents (that is, the value of the services of physical property). Economic historians should find the secular movement of wages relative to rents a rich vein. Showing the symmetry of the institutional changes that follow in the wake of such movements, regardless of the type of government, is one of the major contributions of Slicher Van Bath.[12] We are presently in a long secular period which is running in favor of the economic value of human time.

Clearly, institutional changes that occur in response to the rising economic value of human time call for economic analysis that includes (a) institutional responses to increases in the market price of work, (b) institutional responses to increases in the rate of return to investment in human capital, and (c) institutional responses to increases in consumer disposable income.

Institutional changes in response to increases in wages are predominantly in the realm of internal migration, occupational shifts, and distortions of various sorts. These distortions result in less than optimum job information and less on-the-job training than is consistent with an equalization of the benefits and the costs of such training. In the government's 1967 report, *The People Left Behind*,[13] we have a landmark in analysis with recommendations for lines of public action to improve the institutional performance in this general area.

In approaching the institutional changes related to the rise in the value of human time, the key assumption is that economic modernization is of a type in which production activities require more high skills than they did formerly, and that the demand derived from these activities increases the rate of return to investment in human capital. Again we ask: What are the institutional implications?[14] Looking back, it would appear that our system of education has been flexible. The rub, however, is that it has not performed as well in supplying additional educational services, both quantitatively and qualitatively, for many children of farm families and for large numbers of children of poor families in large cities. In terms of rates of return to investment in poor people, there is a growing body of evidence that supports the inference of a continuing disequilibrium, especially so with respect to elementary and secondary schooling. Higher education is an institution that raises complex and difficult organizational issues. Efficient allocation of resources lags for want of sufficient incentives and information. The self-interest of students is not fully mobilized. The accounting of social benefits (losses) is haphazard, and academic entrepreneurship has all too little opportunity for allocating resources efficiently.

The next chapter examines this and related issues in higher education.

4 Concluding Remarks

When a person has a legal right to the value of the services (products) that are the result of his innate and acquired abilities, he has property rights in his human capital. Slaves who are bound by the institution of slavery have no property rights in their human capital. Legally they are propertyless.

Poor people, who account for most of the world's population, as a rule have some property rights. But their individual human capital component is exceedingly small. The value of the productivity attributed to it is accordingly small.

For individuals and families in high income countries, where large investments in human capital have occurred, the human capital component is large and the value of the productivity attributed to it is large. The rise in the economic value of human time is a key to changes in property rights in human capital.

Many institutional changes in favor of human capital property rights have occurred during recent decades. Their political and legal origins appear to be fairly easy to document. Where the origin has been social, it may be difficult to establish the evidence. There is much to be said for undertaking research to explain these various origins and the economic importance of each. Self-interest should motivate scholars and scientists – including economists – to determine ways and means of extending intellectual property rights beyond existing components, such as patents and copyrights, intellectual facilities and tenure rights, and beyond bare honors to financial rewards.

Not least is the fact that as the economic value of human

time rises, we are in the realm of new and better opportunities. The range of private and social choice is enlarged. It is, indeed, an optimistic set of circumstances that all too few people of the world enjoy. But even so, this favorable type of economic modernization is not without its institutional stresses and strains. Since we can specify and identify these institutional processes we can also analyze the benefits in terms of efficiency, income, and welfare.

Notes and References

1 My first analysis of this issue was in "Institutions, and the Rising Economic Value of Man," *American Journal of Agricultural Economics*, 50 (5), December 1968, 1113–22. I received helpful comments from Earl J. Hamilton, Harry Johnson, and Albert Rees. I am most indebted to Vernon Ruttan for his studies on institutions and for his stress on the human capital property rights issue in my paper. Chapter 4 of my *Investing in People: The Economics of Population Quality*, University of California Press, Berkeley, CA, 1981, pp. 59–84, treats "The Economics of the Value of Human Time."

2 Irving Fisher, *The Nature of Capital and Income*, Macmillan, New York, 1906.

3 John R. Commons, *Legal Foundations of Capitalism*, Macmillan, New York, 1924.

4 Gary S. Becker, "A Theory of the Allocation of Time," *Economic Journal*, 75, September 1965, 493–517.

5 Chapter 12 on the Entrepreneurial Components in Research deals with one important subset of these institutions.

6 C. E. Bishop, "The Urbanization of Rural America: Implications for Agricultural Economics," *Journal of Farm Economics*, 49, December 1967, 999–1008.

7 T. W. Schultz, *Transforming Traditional Agriculture*, Yale University Press, New Haven, CT, 1964.

8 W. David Hopper, "Regional Economic Report on Agriculture," in *Asian Agricultural Survey, Manila*, Asian Development Bank, March 1968, Section 3, vol. 1.

9 T. W. Schultz, "Efficient Allocation of Brains in Modernizing

World Agriculture," *Journal of Farm Economics*, 49, December 1967, 1071–82.

10 Albert Rees called my attention to the fact that courts are more and more explicitly considering earning power in determining the size of the judgments in cases of accidental injury or death.

11 Walter Gellborn, "Poverty and Legality: The Law's Slow Awakening," *Proceedings of the American Philosophical Society*, 112 (2), April 1968, 107–16.

12 B. H. Slicher Van Bath, *The Agrarian History of Western Europe, AD 500–1850*, St Martins Press, New York, 1963.

13 President's National Advisory Commission on Rural Poverty, *The People Left Behind*, Government Printing Office, Washington, DC, September 1967.

14 Professor Earl J. Hamilton reminded me of the insights of Alfred Marshall on some aspects of this issue in chapters 12 and 13 in his *Principles of Economics*, 8th edn, Macmillan, London, 1930.

14

Production of Knowledge by Universities

Scarce resources are required to create, maintain, and distribute the knowledge we have. These knowledge activities have become increasingly more costly. The value of these activities warrants treating them as a specialized economic sector. It is a sector that entails both public and private institutions. Universities are a part of this sector.

This chapter is a critical assessment of the financing of research in a large set of modern universities that are strongly research oriented.[1] A preceding chapter on the entrepreneurial components in organized research is a part of this criticism. So, too, is the chapter on the legal rights issue pertaining to intellectual capital as a part of human capital.

It is no surprise that scholars and scientists are apprehensive of having economics applied to what they do. They may take pride in not being concerned about such mundane affairs as prices, economic productivity, the value of human time, and entrepreneurial functions. They may believe that economics can only debase the pursuit of knowledge.

When a free-lance scholar or scientist pursues knowledge for its own sake at his leisure and at his own expense, it is a private activity. He is not beholden to a university. Universities, however, do not appoint scholars and scientists and pay them salaries to enhance their leisure. Whatever personal satisfactions scholars and scientists derive from their work, the expectations of the university are that they devote a measure of their intellectual endeavors to knowledge activities of the university.

Universities require libraries, laboratories, and other supporting facilities. With few exceptions, neither the faculty nor the complementary personnel are cloistered austere monks or nuns who do their thing for a pittance. Students, governments, foundations, and other patrons foot the bill. Money matters and inflations take their toll. As an institution, universities have special legal privileges and social responsibilities. Freedom of inquiry is both an essential privilege and a serious responsibility of the faculty and students.

Universities, in some respects, are fragile in their knowledge activities. They are vulnerable to interventions by government, to restrictions on grants from foundations, and on funds from private patrons. Caesar is not renowned for providing funds that best serve the knowledge activities of universities. Governments want policy support. Some foundations want policy oriented research that is linked to policy advocacy. Not so long ago, members of the faculty were ever on their guard in keeping trustees from encroaching on their freedom of inquiry. Currently they are complacent, especially so in keeping those who provide public funds for research from impairing their freedom of inquiry.

Fritz Machlup,[2] in his *Production and Distribution of Knowledge*, treats the analytical issues implicit in earnings forgone and other opportunity costs of education. He deals in particular with the vexing issue of whether the benefits from education should be considered "consumption" or "investment," and whether they accrue to students or to others. His analysis is not only formally correct, but refreshingly clear and remarkably all inclusive. His concise treatment of inventive effort and patent protection is a classic and so is his analysis of the complementarity between basic research and higher education.[3]

Machlup's concept of the production and distribution of knowledge includes a wide array of activities in addition to those of universities. His estimates of US expenditures in 1955 using this comprehensive concept totalled $136.4 billion, grouped in the following categories:

Education	$60.2 billion
Research and development	$11.0 billion
Media of communication	$38.3 billion
Information machines	$8.9 billion
Information services	$18.0 billion
	$136.4 billion

What then is there about the issues at hand that go beyond Machlup's studies? He did not deal with the acute tensions between governments and universities, and with the increasing vulnerability of the freedom of inquiry brought about mainly by the intervention of the state.

To say that knowledge is man-made, and that it is a measure of the attainment of any civilization, does not require proof. It is clear to economists that the knowledge activities of research oriented universities are expensive. Scholars and scientists are uneasy about this point.

Some aspects of the distribution of knowledge are not in doubt. Clearly the distribution of knowledge among countries is very unequal. This inequality between countries with low and high incomes *per capita* has been increasing for a long time. Since the forties, however, knowledge pertaining to the improvement of health and to agricultural productivity has become somewhat more equal. Even so, differences in the composition and the general level of knowledge between most poor and rich countries are very large.

It is also evident that the production of knowledge is subject to man-made vicissitudes. When the Cultural Revolution was destroying the universities of China, higher education and research in the United States were flourishing. While China was destroying, India was expanding her universities and now has substantial corps of scientists, engineers, and other classes of highly skilled persons. Meanwhile, the knowledge-producing institutions throughout parts of Africa have been falling apart, as political instability and governmental intervention take their toll.

We are in an era in which the tensions between the university and the state have become increasingly acute.[4] These tensions are worldwide, although they differ greatly among the more than 150 nation-states. In most of them, the intellectual independence of scholarly inquiry is seriously constrained. What most government agencies want is support for their policies and programs, regardless of how harmful these may be.

The pursuit of knowledge is a venture into the unknown. It always entails risk and uncertainty. It was thus for neolithic man and it continues to be so today. Necessity, luck, and ideas tell most of the story. Facing a dwindling supply of food provided by men from hunting, neolithic women invented agriculture and they developed many of the foodcrop species we have today. Our highly skilled plant breeders have produced one new foodcrop species, that is, triticale.[5]

China attained a fairly high state of knowledge and the art of using it many centuries before Europe reached a corresponding level. Chinese farmers used the iron plough, practised crop rotation including multiple cropping, and maintained the productivity of the soil a millennium before European farmers. Anthony Tang,[6] in assessing this legacy of China, shows how striking China's lead was at that time. "The emergence of the new institutions and agents took place in China when Europe was just settling into the 'Dark Age' . . ." Yet despite that large early lead, something went wrong in maintaining and increasing the stock of knowledge, long before the Cultural Revolution in China.

1   *Economic Value of Advances in Knowledge*

Components of additional knowledge are a decisive factor in

economic productivity and welfare. Increases in knowledge that enhance production are an important source of increases in income. But it is not self-evident that this knowledge has the attribute of capital. Knowing that it is a form of capital does not debase its intrinsic worth. On the contrary, this capital attribute increases its value. To reckon this valuable attribute of knowledge, I place a price tag on knowledge. Once we see its economic value, the value of gold is by comparison unimportant.

The quality of both physical and human capital in modern high income countries has, in large measure, originated out of the advances in knowledge.

Increases in the quality of physical capital have originated largely out of advances in knowledge. They made possible the computer, modern communication facilities, and the high-yielding crop varieties. The vast improvements in the quality of most physical capital over time could not have been achieved were it not for advances in knowledge.

The acquired abilities of human beings, the value of which are revealed in wages, salaries, and in their entrepreneurial rewards, along with the additional satisfactions that people derive from their acquired abilities, are forms of human capital. Here, too, and in large measure, the quality of human capital is enhanced over time by advances in knowledge. Engineers who graduate currently will have learned many things in their field of specialization that were not known and therefore not taught to engineers who graduated several decades ago. It is also true for scientists, medical personnel, and economists. Moreover, the stock of human capital has been increasing at a higher rate than that of physical capital.

There is also a component of knowledge that is not embodied in physical capital. Nor is it a part of human capital that can be so identified and measured. It is a form of "common knowledge" that is pervasive in the social environment of a society. It has a value although it is neither private nor public property in any legal sense. It differs greatly between low and high income countries in its composition and in its contribution. It is exceedingly difficult to get an analytical grip on it and to get at the reasons why differences among countries in this form of knowledge persist for long periods of time.

2 Value of the Time of Scholars and Scientists

Life spans become longer, academic careers become more specialized, tenure remains elusive, and mandatory retirement gets set by law. The time span of academic tenure is brief. The economic value of this tenure time of university scholars and scientists matters.

It bears repeating: increases in the value of time of human beings may well be the most distinctive attribute of our type of economy. The hourly wage of production workers in the United States, measured in constant dollars, has risen well over fivefold since 1900. The value of the time of professors also has marched up and up. So has that of women, including housewives, and, not least, the value of the time of students, namely their forgone earnings while they attend college, which now accounts for the largest part of the real costs of their education. We know why our own time has become more valuable, and we also know a good deal about the nature and significance of the resulting income effects on what university scholars and scientists do in allocating their own time. It would be convenient to assume at this point that the tenured faculty of our universities are free agents. It is, of course, true that they are not indentured servants; they are not legally bound to serve the university until they retire. They can leave when they choose; the university, however, is not free to dismiss them. But they are subject to government regulations, increasingly so, the more they are dependent on government funds.

There is another important dimension of time. For a perspective on how very brief our tenure period is, consider the long sense of time suggested by Karl Weintraub, distinguished historian, in his Ryerson Lecture, citing a little story from Hendrik van Loon's *History of Man*: "In a fabled land lies a bald granite mountain. Every hundred years a little bird comes to sharpen its beak by grating it against the mountain. When the bird will have worn down the whole mountain, not even one second of eternity will have passed." It is not surprising that scholars of history and scientists view the economist's concept of time as simply here and now. What a pity that the economist's time is so limited.

Before considering what scholars and scientists do in response to the high value of their time, a review of some issues is called for. It is our good fortune that salaries are high in the United States. Also, there are enough universities to provide a competitive market, acting as the invisible hand in protecting scholars and scientists. The market for the services of scientists is extended by the demand of profit oriented enterprises. Nevertheless, the production and distribution of knowledge in universities are fragile, wherever freedom of inquiry is constrained by government or by patrons. The incentive to acquire the ability to obtain grants for research is strong. Prove that you have that ability and your appointment to permanent tenure is assured! We have Edward Shils's[7] warning, "Woe unto your freedom of inquiry when you sell your intellectual soul to Caesar!"

7   Having High Salaries, What Do They Choose?

Theory implies that the demand for additional time to pursue leisure activities is enhanced by the income effect of higher salaries. What are these leisure activities? If scholars in the humanities were to spend a good bit of their additional leisure-time reading and enjoying the papers and books created by scientists, and if scientists in turn were to find joy in the papers and books of scholars who are not scientists, and both groups revealed their new happiness, it would please even the most critical students. While there is a lack of evidence to assess the implications of a theory of leisure-time, what matters is being free to choose and how scholars and scientists allocate their time.

An important new concept in economics is the permanent income hypothesis advanced by Friedman[8] based on the assumption that both income and consumption are subject to a component of variance. We know that families who derive their income from salaries are favored by a relatively small variance in income. Since university faculty on permanent tenure are thus favored, what is their response? Does it create an incentive to reduce exertion, knowing that the variance in their income will be small? Or is it an incentive to be more adventurous in the research they pursue?

If the salaries of those on permanent tenure were fixed with no increases based on merit, the economic incentive to break new ground would be blunted. On the second issue, evidence from other occupations indicates that having a substantial source of income that is subject to only a small variance is a condition that favors undertaking enterprises with high risk. The corresponding responses of scholars and scientists would be that they also choose to take on research enterprises that entail greater risk, being assured of a steady income.

The faculty and administrators of our universities are dealing with the ever changing research frontier of the sciences and of humanistic scholarship. In addition, they are coping with economic conditions that are also changing. Within our universities, academic entrepreneurship is much more important than is commonly realized. Examine a university within which the available resources are allocated in a purely routine manner over any extended period and you will find that it is on a declining path. University presidents and deans and, to a smaller degree, the overworked heads of departments are as a rule part-time entrepreneurs. Routine teachers are a liability and routine research workers contradict the meaning of research. If, nevertheless, there are such routine teachers and research workers, they are drones.

We need a searching discussion on the persistent dilemma of ever increasing academic specialization. How high is the price of specialization? Most academic economists pay a price for divorcing themselves from history and from the humanities. From Machlup's scholarship, we have a rich vein of information about the knowledge-producing professions in the United States in many branches of learning and departments of erudition.[9] The extent and complexity of the knowledge-producing professions touch on a fundamental issue in the theory of human capital specialization and its productivity. Economists, specialized scholars, and specialized scientists, notwithstanding their professional achievements, are likely to become a nuisance, if not a positive danger, when they make grand pronouncements pertaining to public choices.

High salaries, and living in a country with high income *per capita*, reduce our ability to comprehend the lot of scholars and scientists in countries with low income. It is exceedingly difficult for us who are so very rich to enter into conversations with people who have long been very poor. Even when the same words are used, what they mean to them and to us will be different. There can be no conversation without a language. Moreover, even with a language, we who are rich appear to be incapable of discerning the adverse effects of being poor on the opportunities to do scholarly and scientific work, and on the quality of discussion. Where the government is the controlling Leviathan, we fail to understand how precarious academic activities are, regardless of whether or not there is permanent tenure.

4   Some Implications

No one during Adam Smith's day could have anticipated that human capital would come to dominate – as is the case in the United States. Henry Adams,[10] seeing the United States as it was in 1800, could not have anticipated the extraordinary commitment that its people would make to the promotion of knowledge.

Fritz Machlup has documented the vast array and magnitude of such activities. Why is it that we are not satisfied with our success in creating, promoting, and distributing knowledge? Instead, there is much criticism. Anti-science movements harass scientists and tend to politicize the sciences.[11] Philip Handler,[12] when he was president of the National Academy of Sciences, boldly charged that scientists must expose "the anti-scientific and anti-rationalistic" movements, the "faddist approaches to nutrition," and "unfounded allegations of the environmental hazards." He held that scientists must "unfrock the 'charlatan'" in order to protect the credibility of science, and they must also "contain the feckless debates concerning the magnitude of the risk of innovations and challenge the foolish arguments for a 'risk-free society.'"

Washington is beset with lobbyists who seek to influence public officials regarding legislative appropriations that will favor the special research interests of their clients. Some foundations are doing the research that they want to see performed as an "in-house activity." In this way they establish new policy oriented research areas that they propose to support in awarding grants.

The government has a large measure of monopoly control over basic research. It is wishful thinking to believe that it will fade away. Professor John T. Wilson[13] finds the relationships between the federal government and higher education just short of disastrous. These relationships are greatly impaired in comparison with what they were during the fifties and sixties. Professor Wilson's views are grounded in his experiences as a high official of the National Science Foundation and as president of the University of Chicago.

In an address to the American Philosophical Society on the freedom of inquiry issue, Gerard Piel[14] saw the solution clearly. If the autonomy of American universities is to be secured by public support, the necessary protections cannot be decreed by the executive branch of the federal government. Nor can Congress legislate the guarantee. The autonomy of our universities must be negotiated with the electorate. People must be asked to render their support of the university with their full understanding of its mission. Some significant percentage of the regular voters must be ready to entertain such a proposal, for 30 million college graduates are at large in the population.

The electorate is understandably confused about the value of what academic scholars and scientists do. Scientists, except for those in agricultural research, have done all too little to inform the electorate and to seek its support.

At best our activities in the production of knowledge are fragile. Of course, we are not indentured servants and our salaries are high. There is an ever-present danger, however, of the freedom of inquiry being impaired. The harsh truth is that academic scholars and scientists are not free agents.

Ponder, we must, two of T.S. Eliot's[15] questions: "Where is the wisdom we have lost in knowledge?" and "Where is the knowledge we have lost in information?"

Notes and References

1   I first explored the issues here under consideration in my Franklin Lecture, delivered at Auburn University, Alabama, April 30, 1986; I then extended it in "Are University Scholars and Scientists Free Agents," *Minerva*, 25 (3), 1987, 349–59.

2   Fritz Machlup, *The Production and Distribution of Knowledge in the United States*, Princeton University Press, Princeton, NJ, 1962.

3   Fritz Machlup, *Knowledge: Its Creation, Distribution, and Economic Significance*, vol. 1, *Knowledge and Knowledge Productivity*, Princeton University Press, Princeton, NJ, 1980; also, now, his *The Economics of Information and Human Capital*, Princeton University Press, Princeton, NJ, 1984.

4   Theodore W. Schultz, "Governments, Foundations and the Bias of Research," *Minerva*, 17, Autumn 1979, 459–68.

5   Norman E. Borlaug, "The Green Revolution: Can We Make It Meet Expectations," *Proceedings of the American Phytopathological Society*, III, 1976.

6   Anthony M. Tang, "The Agricultural Legacy," *Conference on Modern Chinese Economic History*, Academia Sinica, Taipei, 1977, pp. 231–50.

7   Edward Shils, " 'Render Unto Caesar . . .': Government, Society and the Universities in their Reciprocal Rights and Duties," *Minerva*, 17, Spring 1979, 129–77.

8   Milton Friedman, *A Theory of The Consumption Function*, Princeton University Press, Princeton, NJ, 1957.

9   Machlup, *Knowledge and Knowledge Productivity; The Branches of Learning*, Princeton University Press, Princeton, NJ, 1982; and *The Economics of Information*.

10 Henry Adams, *The United States in 1800*, Great Seal Books, Cornell University Press, Ithaca, NY, p. 52.

11 Edward Shils, "Science, Faith and the Legitimacy of Science," *Daedalus*, 103, Summer 1974, 1–5.

12 Philip Handler, "The Future of American Science," an address delivered at Illinois Institute of Technology, Chicago, January 29, 1980.

13 John T. Wilson, *Higher Education and the Washington Scene: 1982*, University of Chicago Press, Chicago, IL, 1979.

14 Gerard Piel, "On Promoting Useful Knowledge," *Proceedings of the American Philosophical Society*, 28, December 1979, 337–40.

15 T. S. Eliot, "Choruses 'The Rock'," in *Selected Poems*, The Century Publications 1888–1988, Harcourt Brace Jovanovich, New York, 1930.

15

Entrepreneurial Functions of Families

To examine and explain what individuals and families do in restoring equilibrium continues to be my main purpose.[1] A family is a complex biological, social, legal, and economic entity. A family makes economic decisions. The economic domain of each family is small. They are micro entities. It follows that micro economics is applicable. Micro economics usually has considerable analytical advantage over macro economics in theory that is useful empirically. The complexities of the economics of family behavior pertaining to restoring equilibrium requires further clarification.

Family economics is a new field. As Gary Becker[2] noted, in his American Economic Association presidential address, "modern economists neglected the behavior of families until the 1950s." Since then, major advances in economic knowledge about family behavior have been made. It has become increasingly evident that the family performs important economic functions and that advances in understanding how families behave add a great deal to the core of economics.

The family is not a passive entity. Nor is it an economic robot. It calculates, makes decisions, and takes action. The family deals with changes that originate either from within the family or from outside the family. A placid society, serenely free of disturbing changes, has not been the lot of families.

There are few, if any, families that manage throughout

their life spans to maintain an economic equilibrium at all junctures. It seems inevitable that future families will also be dealing with changes. The observable disequilibria are not restricted to the economic domain since they also occur in the biological, cultural, and legal domains of the family.

The short view of what is happening to the family is heavy with pessimism, stated succinctly by Becker[3] at the outset of *A Treatise on the Family*, "The Family in the Western World has been radically altered, some claim almost destroyed, by events of the last three decades." In his last chapter on "The Evolution of the Family," the long view emerges based on many historical accounts. It implies a strong survival capacity on the part of the family.

Large changes in relative prices of factors and of products are important historical events. Is part of the "fertility transition" a consequence of such events? A study based on 1860–1914 data for Sweden gives an affirmative answer. Would there be a strong survival incentive to sanction polygamy for a generation in a country following a war during which most adult males died? Polygamy occurred in Paraguay following the wars on that country during the eighteen-sixties; it appears that the Church did not oppose it.

Families who are dependent on income that have a large variance (not the families who receive steady wages or salaries with a small variance) are treated in this study, following Friedman,[4] as entrepreneurial families. This subset of families is important. We will examine some of the ways that they deal with disequilibria.

The approach to the economics of the family in most studies that are now a part of the literature in economics does not get at the interactions between the family and the economy as changes occur. It is not that economists who specialize in this part of economics postulate a wholly self-sufficient family; however, with few exceptions, they exclude the entrepreneurial functions of families.

Most of what we want to know about the economics of the

family, in addition to what is now known, are the effects of the performance of the economy on the opportunities, composition, and the economic functions of the family. A part of the supporting argument is that the options, roles, and economic importance of the family are strongly linked to the performance and achievements of the economy over time. The family is not spared from even short periodic changes, be they business cycles, fluctuations in employment, good and bad monsoons (India), or large changes in the rates of economic growth. Studies of long periods of accumulative economic changes, with notable large increases in per capita income, would substantially increase our understanding of families at this juncture.

When we take a long view of changes in the family during which economic possibilities are being extended, we observe that economic specialization produces at a lower cost many of the services that families formerly produced for themselves. Specialization also alters the composition of families. Prime adults, other than wife and husband, leave the family and establish separate households. Increases in family income make it financially possible for parents to support the marriages and the separate households of their children at an age before these offspring can earn enough to do it on their own. The favorable personal income also makes it possible for retired parents to maintain a household that is separate from that of their adult children. Thus, the composition of the family changes when the number of adults who are in it declines as a consequence of the increases in opportunities created by the increases in income from economic modernization.

1   Family Attributes on the Decline

The number of kinfolk attached to the wife–husband family core declines. The economic self-sufficiency of the family declines. The support that adult children provide their parents over the last years of their parents' lives, and also earlier when adversities strike, declines. Since research on these issues is still fragmented, the economic effects of these changes in the family may be viewed as hypotheses. They serve as propositions on a par with the observed worldwide decline of the economic importance of the agricultural sector, and, closely related, the decline in the share of national income derived from the Ricardian "original properties of the soil" in the form of land rent.

Research on the economics of the family has reached the state that it should be possible to give provisional answers to the question, when will each of these particular declines pertaining to the family have completed its downward course? The increase in the fraction of married women who are in the labor force, part or full time, has as yet not peaked. There are no apparent reasons for believing that the value of the time of women will not continue to rise as a consequence of modern economic advances. As the demand for labor requiring brute strength declines and that for skills requiring less physical effort increases, it is plausible that the value productivity of the time of women will rise relative to that of men, and in so doing will narrow the gap in wages or salaries between them. A theory to explain the allocation of time by women to bearing children, household activities (including the rearing of children), and work in the labor market as economic conditions change is not at hand.

The utility implications of these changing conditions await further analysis. Meanwhile, the accumulative increases in personal family income, taking the long view, are likely to continue. With respect to the observable decline in family economic self-sufficiency over time, there is little room for doubt that a careful reckoning would show that families enhance the utility they derive from their increasing dependence on specialization and the market. Fewer kinfolk and less dependence on one's children during old age is also a source of utility.

2   Family and Economy Interactions

The family is not passive on the following issues.

Nuclear versus extended family   The increasing specialization that occurs during economic modernization gives the nuclear family a comparative advantage over the extended family. As the disequilibrium becomes evident, the entrepreneurial ability of families suffices to restore an equilibrium by favoring the nuclear family.

Life span boom   Many families in low income countries find that they are in a state of substantial disequilibrium as a consequence of the large increases in life span.

These recent increases in the length of life must be viewed as an extraordinary achievement. History indicates that, when Western European countries were poor, it took them much longer to achieve these longer life spans than it has in many low income countries since the Second World War. As noted earlier, in India the life expectancy at birth of males increased 43 percent and that of females 41 percent between 1951 and 1971.[5] By 1984, life expectancy at birth of the Indian population was 56 years, as estimated by the World Bank,[6] an increase of 73 percent over that in 1951. India exemplifies this "life span boom" of the last three decades. It has enhanced human well-being, unevenly to be sure. A large part of it has had its origin in advances in knowledge. Families benefited from collective efforts to suppress malaria and to reduce tuberculosis and various endemic diseases. They also benefited from the availability of modern drugs, the service of health centers, improvements in nutrition, and more and better food. Would that we knew: (a) the economic effects on families of the observed decline in the price of an additional year of expected life; (b) the economics of the rate at which families respond to this lower price; and then (c) the economics of the resulting changes in family composition, in age profiles of its members, and in the functions of the family. The "life span boom" has its origin in the decline of the price of attaining a longer life.

Decline in food grain prices   Families as consumers and farm families also as producers have experienced a marked secular decline in real prices, notably so in the case of wheat. Although changes in various commodity prices are important, it is the income effects of wages and salaries that are featured in family economics research, largely for reasons of empirical convenience. Families are not immune, however, to changes in commodity prices, or to changes in rents paid for the use of property (houses, automobiles, household durables), or to changes in prices of services.

Wheat and rice are the world's major food grains. Wheat has become cheaper relative to rice. Half or more of the family income of most rice eaters is spent on food; many, if not most, wheat eaters now spend a very small fraction of their income on wheat for their food. In the United States, less than 16 percent of personal income goes for food in its entirety.

On the London "World Market" during 1867–77, wheat prices exceeded those of rice by 30 percent; by 1911–14, they were about the same. From 1961 to 1972, world wheat prices were half of what was paid for rice.[7,8] The nutritional value per ton of these two food grains is virtually the same. There are two unresolved issues. Why has the cost of producing wheat declined so much more than that of rice? Why has wheat apparently been a weak substitute for rice?

In reckoning the changes in the demand for labor, wheat production has become a man's job; for rice, however, in parts of Asia, where people are poor, much of the work in

planting and harvesting rice is a woman's job. What are
the male and female labor demands and earnings implications? How much of the differences in the world prices of
wheat and rice can be explained by the earnings differences?

*Labor of men and women in corn and milk produc-
tion*   In the United States between 1929 and 1979, the
hours of labor required to produce 100 bushels of corn
dropped from 115 to 3 hours. To produce 100 pounds of
milk labor hours declined from 3.3 hours to 0.3 of an
hour. The deflated corn price declined 30 percent while
milk prices rose 13 percent. Real farm wages rose over
threefold (from $0.49 to $1.59 per hour). There is a very
small demand for farm labor of women in corn production; in milk production (dairy farming), however, the
labor demand for women is sufficient to reduce their
off-farm employment compared with the off-farm employment of women on farms that specialize in producing field
crops. Daniel Sumner's[9] study of off-farm labor supply
and earnings of farm family members, based on a sample
of Illinois farms, shows "that wives of dairy farmers are
less likely to work off the farm than wives on other types
of farms."

3   Linkage Between the Fertility Transition and Changes in Prices

In a recent study, mentioned earlier, based on evidence for
Sweden during 1860–1914, T. Paul Schultz[10] analyzed the
effects of changes in relative prices on the fertility transition.
The evidence shows that the decline in the price of rye relative
to butter led to increases in the wages of women relative to
that of men and to the fertility transition. The conclusion is
that ". . . county level data for this fifty year period in Sweden
suggests that the appreciating value of women's time relative

to men's, played an important role in the Swedish fertility transition, holding constant for real wages of men, child mortality, and urbanization."[11]

4 Family Entrepreneurship and Transitory Income

The relationship between these two concepts was in the forefront in Dorothy Brady's research, and also in the studies by Margaret Reid and by Milton Friedman. Their empirical studies and theory pertaining to permanent and transitory components in family income have received little attention in the research in family economics. It is hard to explain the neglect of Dorothy Brady's[12] studies based on US 1935–6 data covering small cities, villages, and farms. Also neglected is the analysis of the large differences in the transitory component in the income of families in various data sets by Margaret Reid.[13] Even more serious is the neglect of the advance in theory and in empirical work on this issue by Milton Friedman.[14]

As set forth in chapter 10, Dorothy Brady's transitory income is revealed in the changes in assets and liabilities of urban, village, and farm families during 1935–6. Margaret Reid extended the search by examining the behavior of other families at other dates and locations. Milton Friedman[15] drew in part on Brady's and Reid's findings and proceeded to establish a strong linkage between family entrepreneurship and transitory income – namely that the ratio of permanent consumption to permanent income has been decidedly higher for families of wage earners than for entrepreneurial families, and that the difference between entrepreneurial and nonentrepreneurial families in the ratio of permanent consumption to permanent income ". . . seems larger and better established than any other we have examined."

Why is the entrepreneurial role of families comprehended by Brady, Reid, and Friedman, *but* not by most other economists specializing in family economics? The reason is that the analytical approach of Brady, Reid, and Friedman examines family behavior under a much wider all-inclusive set of changes than has been the case in most other studies. Brady, Reid, and Friedman did not exclude events that required entrepreneurship to reestablish an economic equilibrium.

5 Marriage and Children in Entrepreneurial Families

Yue-Chim Wong's[16] studies are based on Hong Kong data. In Hong Kong the overwhelming proportion of family enterprises are exceedingly small. Among men in Wong's sample, there were 1,159 entrepreneurs and 4,121 workers. Among women, there were 647 entrepreneurs and 1,128 workers. Wong found that "Entrepreneurial families derive greater benefits from marriage than worker families. Male entrepreneurs obtain more labor market benefits than workers from marrying well-educated women." He also found that "... children in entrepreneurial households are more likely to work for the family business than as hired labor elsewhere." The value of children is enhanced and the fertility effects are positive.

6 Migration by Families Out of Agriculture

Some occupations are predominantly family affairs. Farming is such an occupation. Few established active farmers are single. The labor in most of agriculture consists of farm family labor. Modern economic growth gives rise to labor disequilibria that require many farm families to migrate out of agriculture. Migrations of families out of agriculture seldom occur evenly over time or evenly by location. Some of these migrations are like small turbulent rivers; others are like large floods.

It bears repeating that migrations of farm families out of agriculture in the United States are pale in comparison with such migrations under way and in prospect in China or in India. Available data for the United States are abundant on this issue.

We know that large spells of migration out of agriculture have not been blissful.[17] They have not been neutral in their economic effects. They did not conform to any knowable expected rate. Economic agents, whether they were rural or urban, policy-makers or economists, could not have foreseen, as of any given date, the full array of changes in economic conditions and the resulting disequilibria that called for reallocation of labor.

As long as modern economic advances continue, the changes in economic conditions that are an integral part of such advances will give rise to disequilibria between farm and nonfarm employment in the allocation of labor. Labor in both sectors becomes increasingly more skilled and more specialized, and the human capital component becomes larger. These changes are important parts of the dynamics of the increasing value of human time.[18]

7 Migration to Reduce Wage Inequalities

In general, wage inequalities between countries increase as a result of unequal rates of economic advances between countries. Since the allocations of capital between countries do not suffice to restore an equilibrium, a special burden falls on labor (individuals and families) to migrate and seek employment in the countries with the higher wages.

During the oil price boom period, when the national income of the oil exporting countries increased greatly, a few of the oil exporting countries permitted foreign labor to enter, and a massive immigration of labor, including many families, occurred. Although Egypt produces some oil, the disequilibrium in real wages between Egypt and oil exporting countries was reduced by a large migration of Egyptian laborers (families) to work in particular oil exporting countries.

There is a long-standing silence in economics on the vast array of economic disequilibria in wages that exists between countries. Governmental controls keep "foreign" labor from entering countries in which high wages prevail. Micro actions by foreign individuals and families are thwarted in their endeavors to equalize wages.

Families in low wage countries engage in extraordinary efforts to establish family networks to circumvent immigration restriction. Such networks are richly documented by Douglas S. Massey[19] in the case of the immigration of Mexicans into the United States. Arrangements to be in the United States at the time when a child is born give the child legal assurance of US citizenship. Various other extraordinary legal, albeit, costly ways are pursued to enter the labor market of the United States.

8   On Personal Distribution of Economic Rewards

A part of the reduction in inequality of the distribution of personal income is a consequence of changes in economic conditions over time. It is this part that is central in my thinking. A decline in the price of food improves the economic lot of poor people more than that of people who are not so poor. In Ricardo's day, the families of laborers gave up half and more of their wages for food. In North America and most of Western Europe, as modernization has proceeded, the fraction of family income spent on food has declined to less than one-fifth of personal family income. Gains in the productivity and economic efficiency of agriculture, for reasons stated earlier, contributed to a reduction in the inequality in the personal distribution of income. The share of national income going to landlords declines as Ricardian land rents become smaller relative to other sources of income.

Here, too, income inequality is reduced. Kuznets takes a long view of the decline in the share of national income derived from property, estimating it to be from about 45 to 25 percent, while labor's part rose from 55 to 75 percent.[20] My hypothesis is that the fivefold increase in real wages per hour of work in the United States since 1900 has dominated the intergeneration personal distributions of income among families. What matters much are the increases in the value of human time over time.

9 Concluding Remark

Producing one's own children is a family matter. The family is not about to fade away. The family in its economic behavior is a flexible and robust entity. By no means have all the recent changes in the family been bad; quite the contrary, most of them are not inconsistent with optimal economic behavior.

While we have learned a great deal from our economic approach to family behavior, it is my contention that our analytical work should be extended to relate economic changes in the rest of the economy to those experienced by the family, exemplified by the "life span revolution" and by large shifts in relative prices in commodities, durables, and services. It is hard to explain the neglect of the highly competent family income studies based on permanent and transitory income concepts. The entrepreneurial behavior of families as they take advantage of economic modernization is essential in restoring equilibrium.

Notes and References

1 This chapter is based in part on my "The Changing Economy and the Family," *Journal of Labor*, 4, part 2, July 1986, 5278–87. I am indebted to Mary Jean Bowman, John Letiche, Margaret Reid, Vernon Ruttan, and T. Paul Schultz for their critical comments.

2   Gary S. Becker, "Family Economics and Macro Behavior," *American Economic Review*, March 1989, 1–13.

3   Gary S. Becker, *A Treatise on the Family*, Harvard University Press, Cambridge, MA, 1981.

4   Milton Friedman, *A Theory of the Consumption Function*, Princeton University Press, Princeton, NJ, 1957.

5   Rati Ram and Theodore W. Schultz, "Life Span, Health, Savings, and Productivity," *Economic Development and Cultural Change*, 27, April 1979, 399–421.

6   *World Development Report, 1986*, issued by the World Bank, Washington, DC, p. 232, Table 27.

7   A. J. H. Latham and Larry Neal, "The International Market in Rice and Wheat, 1868–1914," *The Economic History Review, 2nd series*, 36, May 1983, 260–80, appendix 2, cols B and G. The text shows the market linkages between rice and wheat in India and in London.

8   Theodore W. Schultz, "On Economics and Politics of Agriculture," in *Distortions of Agricultural Incentives*, edited by Theodore W. Schultz, Indiana University Press, Bloomington, IN, 1978, p. 21, appendix A. Updated based on US Department of Agriculture official statistics.

9   Daniel Sumner, "Off-Farm Labor Supply and Earnings of Farm Family Members," Ph.D. Dissertation, Department of Economics, University of Chicago, December 1977.

10 T. Paul Schultz, "Changing World Prices, the Wages of Women and Men, and the Fertility Transition: Sweden 1860–1914," paper presented at the Population Association of America Meeting, Minneapolis, May 4, 1984.

11 Ibid., p. 22.

12 Dorothy S. Brady (senior author), Consumer Purchases Study, Urban, Village and Farm, *Changes in Assets and Liabilities of Families, Five Regions*, Misc. Publ. 464, US Department of Agriculture, 1941, 225 pages. Also, *Family Income and Expenditures, Five Regions, Farm Series*, Misc. Pub. 465, 1941, 366 pages.

13 Margaret G. Reid, "Effect of Income Concept upon Expenditure Curves of Farm Families," *Studies in Income and Wealth*, National Bureau of Economic Research, New York, 1952, vol. 15, pp. 133–74.

14   Friedman, *A Theory of the Consumption Function.*

15   Ibid., p. 227.

16   Yue-Chim Wong, "The Role of Husband's and Wife's Economic Activity Status in the Demand for Children," *Journal of Development Economics*, 25, 1987, 329–52; and "Entrepreneurship, Marriage, and Earnings," *Review of Economics and Statistics*, 68 (4), November 1986, 693–9.

17   Theodore W. Schultz, "Dealing with Economic Imbalances Between Industry and Agriculture," in *The Balance Between Industry and Agriculture in Economic Development*, edited by Kenneth J. Arrow, for The International Economic Association, vol. 1, *Basic Issues*, Macmillan and IEA, New York, pp. 33–48.

18   Theodore W. Schultz, "The Economics of the Value of Human Time," *Investing in People*, University of California Press, Berkeley, CA, 1981, ch. 2.

19   Douglas S. Massey, "Economic Development and International Migration," *Population and Development Review*, 14 (3), September 1988, 386–413. Also, see George J. Borjas and Stephen G. Bronar, "Immigration and the Family," Labor Workshop Paper, April 18, 1989, University of Chicago, including the rich literature on this migration increase, which they cite.

20   Simon Kuznets, *Modern Economic Growth*, Yale University Press, New Haven, CT, 1966; also, my elaboration on Kuznets's analysis in my *Investing in People*, ch. 4, "The Economics of the Value of Human Time," University of California Press, Berkeley, CA, 1981, pp. 59–84.

16

Disequilibria between Industry and Agriculture

How to cope with this class of economic disequilibria is an unsettled policy issue. Seeing what governments do, it could be argued that they are adept at creating such disequilibria. We know many governments pursue policies that distort product and factor values by various means. In many low income countries government specializes in policies that keep agricultural production down; in high income countries many governments do the opposite. Nevertheless, while governments are not blameless, it would be a serious error to attribute all disequilibria of this class to government policy.[1]

I will concentrate on disequilibria that are consequences of economic modernization. The economic events of the last 40 years, the period since the Second World War, will be foremost in my thinking.

For the purpose at hand there are useful studies specializing in international trade, in economic productivity, in agricultural economics, in human capital, and in various other specialties that provide some theory and some evidence pertaining to the sources of economic disequilibria.

I gave considerable thought to these issues in my *Agriculture in an Unstable Economy*,[2] and then with more depth in my *The Economic Organization of Agriculture*.[3] There are qualifications I would want to make about these studies; yet, despite all the changes in economic conditions since then, my principal results continue to be valid. My approach was restricted to the economics of agriculture in a national economy, mainly that of the United States.

Even under the most favorable changes in economic conditions that result in increases in real income, *economic disequilibria are inevitable* and prevention is not the right approach. Surely we do not want to prevent the increasing division of labor and specialization that are an integral part of the process of achieving increases in income. Who among us is set on preventing the increasing returns to be had from specialized physical and human capital? Modernization increases the value of human time and also the real per capita income in many nation-states. It brings about a decline in the share of national income that is accounted for by agricultural land rent. It has contributed to the remarkable increase in life span. If these achievements entail disequilibria, are we to forgo them in order to prevent all disequilibria? The real issue pertains to the incentives that induce economic agents to reallocate the resources in their domain, and to the efficiency of these agents in restoring equilibrium.

If disequilibria cannot be averted and if increases in income are to be had, the focus of policy should be an economic organization that has the best record at inducing economic agents, be they urban or farm people, to equilibrate the economic activities in their domain.

There are changes in economic conditions that create opportunities for more income. Such changes disturb the then prevailing equilibrium and call for a reallocation of resources. For these new opportunities to be realized it is necessary that economic agents perceive that such opportunities are occurring and that they may gain by reallocating the resources in their economic domain. This class of changes in economic conditions occurs unevenly over time. They also occur unevenly by locations. To label such changes in agriculture a *Green Revolution* does not provide any insights into the nature of the disequilibria that occur, or the equilibration that is called for, or the extent to which a worldwide equilibrium has been attained in the distribution and utilization of, for example, high-yielding wheat and rice varieties.

1 Decline in the Value of Agricultural Land

Economic modernization reduces the economic importance of agricultural land. It stands repeating that, contrary to the imprint of Ricardo and Malthus on economic thought, agricultural land rent declines as a fraction of national income. The political influence of landlords also declines. As this transition to a new political balance occurs, there are periods of political instability.

Ricardo's concept of land, "the original and indestructible powers of the soil," is a burden in comprehending the increases in the supply of agricultural land. The supply of such land is not fixed by nature: much of it is a man-made factor of production. It is augmented by investments of various types. Substitutes for land are well illustrated by biological advances in high-yielding varieties of hybrid corn that are fertilizer responsive and disease resistant.

The fate of land is such that it loses its political value as a sinecure of an unprogressive landed aristocracy. What now appears to be a puzzle is the rise in the political influence of farmers in most high income countries. Their political clout increases decidedly, notwithstanding that they and their families have become a small fraction of the population. The land tenure of these farmers varies widely. The rent derived from the productivity of the land becomes smaller relative to that derived from their own labor and equipment and from inputs they purchase from industry.

Governments and international agencies tend to overrate the economic contributions of land and by their actions worsen the land-specific disequilibria. Harrod's[4] big jump in his growth model with no land, however, is premature.

Despite the marked increase in the nominal price of agricultural land during periods of high rates of inflation, my

"The Declining Economic Importance of Agricultural Land"[5] continues to be valid.

2 Economics of Migration

One of the major consequences of economic modernization is that many people leave agriculture. These movements of people are responses by farm people who perceive that the value of time working in agriculture declines relative to that in industry. Where the option of leaving agriculture is not foreclosed by policy, many farm people choose not to stay down on the farm.

These movements of people out of agriculture are driven by disequilibria in earnings from work. These movements seldom occur evenly over time or evenly by locations. Most are small; some, however, are massive movements.

The *World Development Report 1986*[6] classifies 36 countries as low income economies. As of 1980, 70 percent of the labor force in these countries were in agriculture. As a statistic it stood at 987 million agricultural workers. China and India accounted for three-quarters of this enormous number of laborers, ages 15–64, in agriculture. Worldwide, over half of the 128 countries listed by the World Bank had less than half of their labor in agriculture; 37 countries had less than a fourth and 18 countries had less than a tenth of their labor in agriculture.

If the labor force in Chinese agriculture in 1980 had been down to half of the national total, there would have been 126 million fewer laborers in agriculture. If the modernization of agriculture in China were to proceed during the next several decades as it has in recent years, the prospects would be that the labor requirements of agriculture in China could well be down to half of the total labor force of China. Ponder the immense reallocations of labor in China resulting in her achieving a *new* economic equilibrium implied by such prospects. Meanwhile, policies have long been set against movements of labor by severe restrictions on the movement of rural people into cities in China. The gap in earnings between city and rural labor increased as a consequence. The household responsibility system, an important new economic organizational approach to agricultural production, as Justin Lin[7] has shown, is reducing the labor requirements of agriculture substantially.

Although movements of labor out of agriculture within the United States pale in comparison with the prospective movements in China or in India, I turn to them because the available data show how very uneven the movements have been. These movements of farm people out of agriculture since 1930 did not conform to any knowable expected rate. Economic agents, whether they were rural or urban, or policy-makers, or economists, could not have foreseen at any given date the full array of changes in economic conditions and the resulting disequilibria that called for reallocation of labor.

The Great Depression reversed this movement, and a net movement into agriculture occurred during 1932 and 1933. Although the increases resulting from net changes in births and deaths within the farm population were appreciable, the labor force in agriculture declined from over 10 million in 1930 to 3.2 million in 1985. The annual net movement of people out of agriculture ranged from a half to eight-tenths of a million during 1936–40. In 1943 it was well over 3 million. In 1946 the movement reversed once again. From 1948 to 1970 there were nine scattered years when the net out-movement ranged between 1 million and 2.2 million.[8] To summarize, in 1930 the farm population count was 30.5 million. The natural increase of births over deaths in the farm population was about 12 million during the period between 1930 and 1985. Had there been no out-movement and adding the natural increase and with a bit of fancy arithmetic, the 1985 farm population would have been 42.5 million. The actual farm population in 1985 was down to 5.3 million, which implies a net out-movement of over 37 million.

As long as economic modernization continues, the changes in economic conditions that are an integral part of it will give rise to disequilibria between industry and agriculture in the allocation of labor. Labor in both sectors becomes increasingly more skilled and more specialized, and the human capital component becomes larger. These changes are important parts of the explanation of the increasing value of human time.[9]

3 Upsurge in Life Expectancy

Gains in the state of health that account for longer life spans increase the lifetime productivity of workers as a consequence of their longer participation in the labor force, their greater physical ability to do work, and the smaller loss of working time because of illness. In many low income economies, investments in health account in large measure for the recent remarkable increases in life span. I turn to the first-rate Indian data. The 1951 Census gives the life expectancy at birth of males at 32.4 years and for females at 31.7 years.[10] As of 1984 it was 56 and 55 years respectively – a 73 percent increase in 33 years. People in Western Europe and North America at no time attained anywhere near as large an increase in life expectancy in so short a period.

Longer life expectations make it worthwhile to acquire more schooling and more on-the-job experience as investments in future earnings.

Improvements in the state of health occur very unevenly, especially in the case of agriculture in low income countries. The effects of this unevenness in health on the productivity of agricultural labor have not gone unnoticed. My quote[11] pertains to India.

> Public health programs initiated during the first five-year plan (1951–56) and carried on through the second plan (1956–61) had a much larger favorable effect on health than did the

programs undertaken later. The program to suppress malaria tells the story. Official data indicate that the incidence of malaria dropped from 73 million cases in 1952–53 to about 1.1 million in 1959–60. But the malaria program suffered a setback in 1965.

Differences within India in the decline in mortality alone explain about 28 percent of the interstate variations in agricultural productivity. The fall and rise of malaria among districts provide an additional test of the effects of health on productivity.

The economics of health in low income countries has received all too little attention. Health is a component of human capital. Once a (much) higher life expectancy is attained, traditional family human capital no longer suffices. Additional and new forms of human capital are required to equilibrate the investment opportunities and thus establish a new and more productive equilibrium. Furthermore, as Usher[12] has shown, the value of the additional utility that people derive from improvements in health, especially in low income countries, implies that the real rate of increases in income has been appreciably higher than that reported in the national statistics of these countries.

4 Industry becomes the Major Supplier of Agricultural Inputs

The modernization of agriculture entails ever more inputs that are purchased from nonfarm sectors. These inputs are major carriers of elements of the technical advances in agriculture. Here, too, disequilibria abound, as noted in earlier chapters.

These purchased agricultural inputs are a part of the intriguing story of increasing productivity events. There are periods when output per acre, per man-hour, and per unit of "capital" all increase.

Another part of this story is based on the fact that, before new and better agricultural inputs can be created, specialized human capital is required to create them. Growth economists who deal with the changes in technology usually fail to see that specialized human capital is a prerequisite, exemplified by what plant breeders do when they create a new high-yielding crop variety. Specialized human capital is one of the essential components for doing this research.

The public sector continues to play a major role in agricultural research. It has been propelled throughout the world, very unevenly however. The perceived high rate of return, supported by many studies, provided strong incentives to expand. Large as public sector agricultural research has become, it still has not arrived at an equilibrium viewed as an investment.

Scientist man-years serve as a measure of the specialized human capital involved in agricultural research. Scientists engaged in agricultural research in the public sector worldwide increased over threefold from 1959 to 1980 (from 47,000 to 148,000). Total expenditure in constant 1980 US dollars increased from $2 billion to $7.4 billion.

Much of what we have learned about human capital can be stated briefly as follows.

1 The human capital that people in high income modern economies have accumulated consists of a great deal of specialized human capital.
2 A Crusoe, or a self-sufficient farm family, or a small population on a small island with no trade with people at any other location, has little or no incentive to acquire specialized human capital.
3 During economic modernization the rate of increase in human capital is higher than that of reproducible physical capital.
4 Human capital enhances the productivity of both labor and physical capital.
5 People at each skill level are more productive in a

high human capital environment than in one that is low in human capital.

6 Adam Smith's famous theorem that the division of labor depends on the extent of the market encompasses the advantages of specialization, including the gains from specialized human capital.

Despite folklore that agriculture is immune to specialization that requires specific human capital, today's modern farmer is increasingly dependent on specialized human capital.

5   Restoring Equilibrium

It is all too convenient to assume that there is a strong tendency toward equilibrium and let it go at that. (We need to ascertain what are the costs of equilibrating and what are the gains.) Is the prevailing economic organization conducive to efficiency in restoring equilibrium?

Under what circumstances and at what rate do farmers and other private economic agents march to the beat of the general equilibrium drummer, as we do analytically? The adoption of the high-yielding wheat by farmers in India was not motivated to bring the Indian wheat economy into equilibrium. It was the profitability of the higher yielding wheat that induced the adoptions.

Profits did the trick despite the then strong view held by many in India that profitability was the wrong game. The prevailing doctrine was that small, poor, private farmers were immune to profits. I protested against the view then and I continue to do so.

But under what conditions are profits efficient in dealing with economic disequilibria? Surely not in a regime in which ambiguities abound as a consequence of procurement quotas, subsidized agricultural inputs, controlled farm prices, and all manner of regulations.

There are economic organizational choices for dealing with disequilibria. As a subsector, agricultural research has evolved a fairly efficient decentralized type of organization to take advantage of new research opportunities. Farms, however, are too small to do it. In low income economies private industries that produce agricultural inputs account for a small part of the on-going agricultural research. Most of it, as a worldwide activity, is being done in the public sector. Economists are doing their homework on these issues and on prospective research opportunities. The record of the success in this activity since 1950 is strong and clear.

The economic organization that prevails in most low income countries results in underinvestment in various dimensions of human capital. Specialized human capital includes proficiency in a language. My reasons for attributing a great deal of economic importance to primary schooling are as follows.

1   The acquired abilities to *read* efficiently and to *write* with competence are important in achieving economic modernization, and they are in general necessary prerequisites to investing in additional specialized human capital. Once again I call attention to the useful historical perspective on literacy now available from Jeffrey Brooks's[13] *When Russia Learned to Read*.

2   The real costs of learning to read and write are at their lowest during the early years of primary schooling; these costs increase as the value of time of the maturing student rises.

3   The abilities to read and write are critical components of the quality of human capital of any population.

All this is well known, but investment disequilibria pertaining to primary schooling are chronic in many low income countries. Parents cannot come up with the required funds.

Nor can their governments acquire funds by borrowing capital in international markets for this purpose, despite strong evidence that the rates of return to investment in primary schooling are, in general, higher than those in secondary schooling or in higher education, and that they also tend to exceed the normal rates of return to investments in physical capital.

Banks, however, are not in the business of providing funds for primary schooling. For banks human capital is a fancy idea that is harmless when it is confined to the ivory tower. On this score the World Bank is no exception; human capital is deemed to be all too intangible to qualify, no matter how high the projected prospective rates of return may be.

The World Bank, however, is not restricted to making hard loans. It has the International Development Association (IDA) which is a large window for doing soft financial business. IDA credits are so soft that for all practical purposes they are "free funds," provided that the country receiving IDA funds does not reckon the political costs of getting them.

IDA credits beginning in 1961 and through 1982 (the last year for which I[14] have figures) totaled $26.7 billion, which amounted to $43 billion in 1982 dollars. Less than 6 percent of these credits were allocated to education. As far as one can tell, very little indeed was used to increase the stock of human capital that primary schooling creates.

In the case of physical capital the legal and institutional foundation of private property has evolved over centuries of experience. Specialized human capital which is private has no comparable foundation. Plant breeders, chemists, and other scientists are not protected from time clocks, from mandatory retirement regardless of productivity, and from being organized as if their work were routine. To patent the fruit from specialized human capital is a fragile part of the required foundation.

6 Lastly

My conclusions pertain to economic disequilibria between industry and agriculture that occur as a consequence of economic modernization. I have not dealt with what governments do. Although many governments are adept at creating economic disequilibria, few concentrate on improvements in economic organization to enhance the ability and efficiency of private economic agents in their endeavors to cope with disequilibria.

Many nation-states pursue policies that distort world trade and thereby reduce the gains to be had from trade. Nation-states in this and in other ways reduce specialization, reduce productivity, and reduce the rate of increases in income.

Economic organization can be improved to take prompt and full advantage of the decline in the economic importance of agricultural land. Improvements in economic organization are also required to enhance the abilities of farm people by additional investments in schooling and health which would improve the reallocation process.

We know the extent of the successful distribution and utilization of the new high-yielding wheat and rice varieties throughout the world. But we do not know the nature and significance of the disequilibria that have occurred, or the equilibration that has taken place, or the extent to which a worldwide new equilibrium has been attained in the production and consumption of wheat and rice.

Prevention of disequilibria that occur during economic modernization is the wrong issue. The issue that matters pertains to incentives that are efficient at inducing private economic agents to reallocate their resources and thus contribute to the establishment of a new and more productive equilibrium.

The capital markets, including banks, are not organized to provide funds for investing in human capital. The World

Bank is no exception. IDA credits distributed by the Bank are for all practical purposes "free," that is, costless. All too few of these billions of dollars are being invested in human capital.

Notes and References

1   Based mainly on my article "Dealing with Economic Imbalances Between Industry and Agriculture," in *The Balance Between Industry and Agriculture in Economic Development*, edited by Kenneth J. Arrow, for the International Economic Association, vol. 1, *Basic Issues*, Macmillan and IEA, New York, 1988, pp. 33–48.

2   Theodore W. Schultz, *Agriculture in an Unstable Economy*, McGraw-Hill, New York, 1945.

3   Theodore W. Schultz, *The Economic Organization of Agriculture*, McGraw-Hill, New York, 1953.

4   R. F. Harrod, *Towards a Dynamic Economics*, Macmillan, London, 1948.

5   Theodore W. Schultz, "The Declining Economic Importance of Agricultural Lands," *Economic Journal*, 61, December 1951, 725–40.

6   World Bank, *World Development Report 1986*, Oxford University Press for the World Bank, New York, 1986.

7   Justin Lin, "The Household Responsibility System in China's Agricultural Reform: A Study of the Causes and Effects of an Institutional Change," Ph.D. Dissertation, University of Chicago, April 1986.

8   US Department of Commerce, Bureau of the Census, *Historical Statistics of the United States*, part I, table series c76–80, "Estimated Annual Movement of the Farm Population: 1920–1970," Washington, DC, 1975, p. 96.

9   Theodore W. Schultz, "The Economics of the Value of Human Time," *Investing in People*, University of California Press, Berkeley, CA, 1980, ch. 4, pp. 59–84.

10 Rati Ram and Theodore W. Schultz, "Life Span, Health, Savings and Productivity," *Economic Development and Cultural Change*, 27, April 1979, 399–421.

11 Theodore W. Schultz, "Investment in Population Quality," *Investing in People*, University of California Press, Berkeley, CA, 1980, ch. 2, p. 38.
12 D. Usher, "An Imputation to the Measure of Economic Growth for Changes in Life Expectancy," edited by M. Moss, *The Measurement of Economic and Social Performances*, National Bureau of Economic Research, New York, 1978, pp. 193–226.
13 Jeffrey Brooks, *When Russia Learned to Read: Literacy and Popular Literature: 1861–1917*, Princeton University Press, Princeton, NJ, 1985.
14 Theodore W. Schultz, "Investing in People: Schooling in Low Income Countries," presented at the World Bank's Education Staff Retreat, January 10, 1986.

17

Human Capital in the Modernizing Economy

This closing chapter is an extended summary of our results. We found that the scope and substance of human capital explain in large measure economic modernization. In Faulkner's words, "Man without skills and knowledge leans terrifically against nothing."

New specialized forms of human capital are basic components in economic modernization. They augment income. In doing so they create economic disequilibria. There are also forms of human capital that serve to restore economic equilibrium.

Endeavors to identify and measure the changes in transitory and permanent components of income and to explain the aggregate increases in national income are as yet far from adequate, mainly because of the limitations of economic knowledge about changes in economic conditions over time.

What has emerged, however, is a substantial consensus in economics on major sources of increases in national income. We may be well advised to concentrate our analytical work on the following overlapping sources, treating them as economic events: (a) advances in technology; (b) proliferation of human capital; (c) increases in specialization; and (d) additional specialization induced by the increases in income derived from (a), (b), and (c). As these increases in income are attained, disequilibria occur and additional income is derived from restoring equilibrium.

I begin with a modest critique of the first four overlapping sources of increases in income. I then concentrate on the role of human capital in restoring equilibrium.

1 Advances in Technology

Advances in technology are endogenous events. These advances are man-made. They originate from within the economy. As noted at the outset of this study, neither the sun, the earth, the wind, nor El Niño is in the business of developing new and better technology. The analytics of endogenizing technology is now the preferred treatment.

In retrospect, it seems odd that early growth models treated technology as being exogenous. What seems even more peculiar is that now, in designing models to endogenize technology, there appears to be a lack of awareness of the published contributions on theory with evidence pertaining to this approach. The analytics of endogenizing advances in technology, including robust estimates of costs, social returns, and gains in welfare, were published over 30 years ago by Zvi Griliches.[1] His classic study paved the way for a considerable number of comparable economic studies of advances in technology.

We have learned that it may take many years before returns from higher yielding crops are realized, as was the case in hybrid corn. Recall that a theory of hybridization dates back to 1905. Hybrid corn research began in 1910. It took 23 years of organized research to create the first hybrid seed released to be used. As a technological advance, hybrid corn is a great economic success story. It includes the value of the output from the cropland released from corn, the reductions in the costs of feed to produce livestock products, and the *resulting consumer surpluses*. These are all changes that occurred inside the economy. They are basic economic sources that give rise to increases in income.

The costs of technological failures must also be reckoned.

The high-yielding wheat that India imported in the mid-sixties was created by highly competent specialized plant breeders in Mexico. India's wheat production sky rocketed from 11 to 46 million tons by 1984. We await a theory of economic productivity to rationalize this extraordinary event.

It stands repeating that the spark that ignited the Green Revolution in wheat in India had its origin in the International Center for Improvement of Maize and Wheat (CIMMYT). It entailed years of costly research. CIMMYT's high-yielding wheat originated from inside the international economy. It was man-made and so were each of the complementary inputs that were required to produce the high wheat yields in India.

We are now back on the right track analytically in dealing with advances in technology. It is reassuring. We will discover, however, that it is a daunting analytical task. It entails both micro and macro entities. In the corn research example, large long-term investments were required. The highly skilled scientists and their research laboratories and experiment stations are costly. Corn is grown in many different countries. Hybrid corn seed is decidedly location specific. Scale issues are complex. Within the United States the corn-producing areas are not homogeneous. Each of the many geographical locations requires a specific hybrid designed for the particular area. Most organized research pertaining to hybrid corn is geographically specific and scale limitations dominate.

How much analytical guidance can be had from existing economic models designed to explain and account for the aggregate part of the country's national income that originates from all advances in technology over a period of decades? To do this is as yet beyond the capacity of our theory and evidence.

We must for the time being settle for less, but even that is formidable, unless there is some way of aggregating all such advances in technology into a single "homogeneous" economic entity.

In addition to the unsettled issues pertaining to increases in income from advances in technology, evidence and reason lend support for an approach that treats specialization as the primary explanation of increases in income.

2   Proliferation of Human Capital

In the modernizing economy, most of the increases in income originate out of the proliferation of human capital. We must hold fast to specialized human capital. We must develop theory to analyze the interactions of physical and human capital accumulations that induce investment in specialized human capital. Is it possible to identify the *external effects* of human capital postulated by Lucas?[2] These effects spill over from one person to another. People at each skill level are more productive in high than in low human capital environments. Human capital enhances the productivity of both labor and physical capital. Lucas sees "human capital accumulation as a *social* activity, involving *groups* of people, in a way that has no counterpart in the accumulation of physical capital."

3   Specialization and Income Increases

The vast extent of modern economic specialization should give us pause to reflect. If we knew the economics of this vast specialization, we would know much of the economics that matters in achieving increases in income. Growth models do not give us that knowledge.

Specialization abounds in our factories, commerce, manufacturing, and in light and heavy industries. But what about the professions? I turn to the production and distribution of knowledge in the United States based on the studies by Machlup.[3] He shows that much specialization prevails. Machlup's last book is on the economics of information and human capital. It is evident that the extent and complexity of our knowledge-producing professions bespeak *human capital specialization* and it accounts for much of the realized productivity.

Clearly, as has been stressed in this study, agriculture is not immune to specialization. As noted earlier, it is exemplified by corn belt farm families who no longer produce eggs, milk, vegetables, and fruit for their home consumption. Meat is also purchased. So is the electricity, gas for fuel, and telephone service. The farmer no longer produces his own seed corn. He buys hybrid seed appropriate to his area. His production expenses are large; they consist mainly of inputs produced by industry. Pig production is highly specialized into (a) producing breeding stock, (b) farrowing to weaning, (c) producing feeder pigs, and lastly (d) finishing their growth to suit market demands. Yet the myth persists that there is virtually no specialized physical and human capital within agriculture.

The gains from two-way trade in similar products between similar countries is a received part of international trade studies. Becker[4] applies the same economic logic to the division of labor within the household. Members of the household specialize their investments and time. "Moreover, with constant or increasing returns to scale, *all* members of efficient households must be completely specialized." Becker sees increasing returns from specialized human capital as a strong force creating a division of labor in the allocation of time and investments in human capital between married men and married women.

Rosen[5] is both cogent and concise on specialization in his analysis cited earlier in this study, to wit: "Incentives for specialization, trade, and the production of comparative advantage through investment are shown to arise from increasing returns to utilization. Hence, the rate of return is increasing in utilization and is maximized by utilizing specialized skills as intensively as possible. Identically endowed individuals have incentives to specialize their investments in skills and trade with each other for this reason, even if production technology exhibits constant returns to scale. The enormous productivity and complexity of modern economies are in good measure attributable to specialization."

The idea of increases in returns had considerable influence on the thinking of the early economists. The origins of such returns were perceived mainly as historical events, not as analytical implications derived from theory. Allyn Young,[6] in his "Increasing Returns and Economic Progress," made an important analytical contribution. But his contribution has long been neglected.

Young extended the then available theory so that economists could pursue increases in returns. It should have made room for economic events that result in increases in output that exceed the increases in inputs. Did Young turn economists off by asserting "I suspect, indeed, that the apparatus which economists have built ... may stand in the way of a clear view of the more general or elementary aspects of the phenomena of increasing returns..."?

Some of the pertinent ideas of economists, before growth models became popular, had a comprehensiveness that has been lost in today's economics. What has not been lost fortunately is the magnificent idea pertaining to the division of labor, its origin, and its income-producing capacity. Even so, the economic importance of the division of labor is presently underrated. It holds one of the keys to specialization, to investment in specialized human capital, and to classes of increasing-income events. But there is too little room in today's growth models even for Adam Smith's division of labor. Nor is there room for Marshall's laws[7] of increasing returns. In the same vein, it is hard to explain the long silent treatment by economists of Young's classic paper.

Part of the explanation for this neglect of so fruitful a concept surely stems from the growing technical refinement of economics, which brings with it a desire for ever greater precision in the use of terms. As economics has become ever more rigorously and minutely exact, the richness of the idea of increases in returns has eroded.

When the early English economists observed the high rates of increases in production by various manufacturing industries, they attributed a part of the additional income to increases in returns. The favorable changes in economic conditions in their day came to be known as the Industrial Revolution. As an economic process it had much in common with what is now referred to as the Green Revolution in agriculture.

Marshall argued that "the part which nature plays in production shows a tendency to diminishing returns, [while] the part which man plays shows a tendency to increasing returns. . . ." Man's part in agriculture conforms to the law of increasing returns. Marshall's insights are increasingly valid as economic modernization is being achieved.

Advances in technology, innovations, discoveries, and other sources of increases in income episodes are economic events. Most of them are small micro events, as in the case of a farmer's increase in corn yields made possible by hybrid seed. Such events can, as a rule, be identified and measured. Their economic effects are in general ascertainable. But when increases in income are attributed to large "macro events" – the Industrial Revolution, for example – the specific sources of the increases in incomes are difficult to isolate and measure.

In the micro domain, in which individuals and families make allocative decisions, their response to economic disequilibria that occur as a consequence of economic modernization is to restore the equilibrium in their own domain.

Nature, as Marshall had perceived it, is a minor source of these income-increasing events. For most analytical purposes they are consequences of the activities of human beings. They may have their origin either from within or outside the economic system. Those that originate from within would be included in Schumpeter's theory of economic development.

These income-increasing events have become important sources of additional income streams. These events spawn related events. The economy of many countries has a built-in capacity to create income-increasing entities notably by means of organized research, research and development in general, university based science research, investment in education, and investment in the distribution of knowledge.

The idea of such events conjures up the old ideological issue of a *surplus* that is *unearned*. It is a false issue. This class of events accounts for most increases in income and in welfare.

4   Human Capital in Restoring Equilibrium

The ability of individuals and families to restore equilibrium in their private economic domain is enhanced by the quantity and quality of their human capital. The economics of restoring equilibrium is in general neglected in economics. Schumpeter's approach to economic development is a notable exception.

5   Limitations of the Tendency Assumption

When a disequilibrium occurs, it may be treated by means of special assumptions. The standard treatment is to rely on the *tendency assumption*, based on the proposition that there is such a tendency throughout the economy. As noted in chapters 1 and 2, that such a tendency of sorts exists is not at issue. If it is a strong tendency, there is merit in using this assumption to simplify the analytical task. If, however, it is not a strong tendency, the analyst is in trouble. We cited Knight[8] and Boulding[9] in support of the tendency assumption. We then turned to Hicks[10] on what is at issue. His argument is telling. "Something has to be specified about reactions to disequilibrium before the existence of a tendency to equilibrium can be asserted.... Even if the equilibrium exists, and the tendency to equilibrium exists, we may still have insufficient ground to justify the equilibrium assumption if the convergence to equilibrium is very slow."

6   Micro Evidence

We now have many studies that show the magnitude of the positive effects of experience, training, schooling, advanced education, and the state of health on allocative efficiency in restoring equilibrium.

Analysis of restoring equilibrium entails both macro and micro theory. It may also entail the effects of institutions and of policy. The reason for concentrating on the micro part is that its implications are more readily testable than those derived from macro theory. It is so empirically because of the greater divisibility of the entities inherent in micro economics. What individuals and families do within firms and households, or who are self-employed, gives rise to many sets of data. For example, the effects of the schooling of farmers in various parts of the world on their success, as they take advantage of a new high-yielding crop variety, tell a consistent story. Thus, a consensus emerges that schooling increases the rate of adoption of high-yielding crop varieties by a rate that can be measured.

The economic domain of my human agent is small. There is ample hard evidence that shows that, when this agent perceives that he is no longer allocatively efficient because of a change in conditions, he acts to bring his small domain into equilibrium. What he does is treated here as entrepreneurship. The motive of this entrepreneur is not that of restoring a general economic equilibrium. He is concerned about the disequilibria in his own private domain.

With respect to the opportunities that are available to small entrepreneurs, much depends on the prevailing national organization of the economy. There is strong evidence that choice of organization matters greatly.

Policy oriented economic inquiry understandably searches for ways of preventing disequilibria that occur as a consequence of economic modernization. Leaving the organizational choice between a centrally controlled and a market oriented economy aside, are there ways that a market oriented economy could prevent all micro disequilibria? All indications are that it is not possible to attain the increases in income to be had from economic modernization without disequilibria occurring. A centrally controlling economy may try to conceal such disequilibria but it too cannot keep them from occurring.

The innate and acquired abilities of people, be they individuals or families in charge of firms or households, or who are self-employed, are exceedingly important in restoring equilibrium. Human capital inquiry to ascertain the economic value of work experience, schooling, more education, and health has added substantially to our knowledge of economic value of these human capital components.

7   Search for Entrepreneurs

Entrepreneurs are not accorded the status of an occupation. Useful entrepreneurial statistics are rare. Reported wages, salaries, and other earnings for work do not give us entrepreneurial earnings. What entrepreneurs earn is not identified in national income accounting. Nor are their earnings identified in micro empirical studies using standard production function techniques, which as a rule report a residual. However, whether part of the residual may be entrepreneurial earnings is left undetermined. Chapters 3, 4, and 5 treat various attributes and functions of entrepreneurs in a modernizing economy. We do not feature the coordination of the factors of production within the firm under a state of equilibrium as Coase has done. Coase's entrepreneur exists in a market economy that is in equilibrium.

Like intelligence, entrepreneurial ability is one of the general attributes of the human population. Observable human behavior in response to changes in economic conditions indicates that most able-bodied adults do what is here deemed to be entrepreneurship. They break their routine and proceed to reallocate their own time and related resources when they perceive that it is worthwhile to do so. The implication is that not only individuals who are in charge of business firms and farmers so respond, but also others who are in self-employed occupations, employed workers, students, and women who are in charge of households have the abilities to be entrepreneurs. But these entrepreneurial skills differ for reasons of given genetic abilities and acquired abilities.

On changes in the production function, Becker[11] is clear and concise: "As conditions improve – as knowledge expands – the function 'shifts' and a larger useful output is obtainable from the same inputs. Even at a moment of time, the functions vary ... as 'entrepreneurial' knowledge and the nature of the product vary." Furthermore, "The level of technology varies ... among firms in the same industry because of differences in entrepreneurial ability...." The entrepreneur's stock of knowledge in this context is a proxy for his ability.

Although genetic abilities of entrepreneurs vary and the differences in abilities on this score may matter, we have concentrated on acquired abilities because, as far as we know, the distribution of genetic abilities within large populations is about the same. Thus, it is plausible that there is no appreciable difference in the level and distribution of genetic abilities between the people of China and of the United States. But the per capita acquired abilities are decidedly less in China than in the United States. For individuals in a market regime, for any past or present date, it is useful to think in terms of a supply of entrepreneurial ability. Each individual has his own "private" supply curve which declines initially, as Becker[12] has noted, ". . . because of the fixed cost of using the entrepreneur's own time and related resources. Eventually, it rises because the opportunity cost of a single owner's time increases as he is forced to draw more and more on leisure and sleeping time. . . ." Full-time entrepreneurship, however, is exceedingly rare.

On the supply of acquired abilities, the best studies to date pertain to education as forms of human capital.

8   Education and Entrepreneurship

The productivity of US agriculture provides strong evidence that education enhances the entrepreneurial ability of farmers. The empirical results are not restricted to differences in the effects between 8 and 12 years of schooling on the allocative ability of farmers. The evidence also resolves the puzzle why the proportion of US farmers with a college education is increasing. Farmers are normally both self-employed workers and entrepreneurs. Thus the productivity effects of education are of two parts, namely on work skills and on entrepreneurship in dealing with the disequilibria that occur as a consequence of changes in the economy. In *Transforming Traditional Agriculture*, I advanced the hypothesis that the schooling of farmers increases their allocative ability. This hypothesis led to many studies to determine the effects of schooling on the adoption of new superior agricultural inputs. Chaudhri[13] was among the vanguard in showing that changes made in the composition of agricultural inputs is sensitive to the schooling of farmers. Research in this area owes much to Welch,[14] Griliches,[15] and Evenson.[16] In Welch's approach, the demand for entrepreneurship is estimated by the level of agricultural research activity. He found that college graduates increased their earnings 62 percent more than those who had completed high school.

Huffman's[17] studies got at the heart of the allocation issue.

The details appear in a note in the reference.

Petzel's[18] study deals with the relationships between the education of farmers and the dynamics of acreage allocations to soybean production in the United States. His study focuses on a period of rapid growth in the acreage devoted to soybeans in nine states from 1948 to 1973. Petzel found that the adjustments made by farmers occurred more rapidly in the counties where average education levels are highest. He also found more rapid adjustments with respect to two dimensions of scale, namely the total crop area devoted to soybeans and the unit scale per farm.

There are few economic regularities that are as valid empirically as is the proposition that the entrepreneurial ability of farmers is enhanced by their education. At hand are the results of a comprehensive survey of the effects of farmers' education on their performance in modernizing agriculture, which includes 20 low income countries, by Dean T. Jamison and Lawrence J. Lau.[19] It is hard to resist their finds!

9 *Property Rights in Human Capital*

As noted in chapters 1 and 13, people who are bound by the institution of slavery have no property rights in their human capital. Poor people, who account for most of the world's population, in general have some property rights. However, their individual human capital component is very small. In high income countries where investments in human capital have been large, and where the rise in the value of human time has been pronounced, we observe that the property rights of people in their human capital is being enlarged and protected.

In the United States and also in other countries where wages, salaries, and earnings of entrepreneurs account for three-fourths and more of personal income, important institutional changes in favor of human capital property rights have occurred during recent decades. The political and legal origins of these changes appear to be fairly easy to document. Where the origin has been social, it may be difficult to establish the evidence. There is much to be said for undertaking research to analyze the various origins and the economic importance of each. Self-interest should motivate scholars, scientists, including economists, to determine ways and means of extending intellectual property rights going beyond existing patents and copyrights, beyond existing safety in the work place, beyond tenure rights, and beyond honors to additional financial rewards for various unprotected intellectual property rights.

As the economic value of human time rises, we are in the realm of new and greater opportunities. The range of private and social choice is enlarged. It is, indeed, an optimistic set of circumstances that all too few people of the world enjoy. But even so, our favorable circumstances are not free of institutional stresses and strains. Since we can specify and identify these institutional processes we can also analyze their results in terms of efficiency, income, and welfare.

What was foretold in chapter 1 is now in hand. Advances in technology and acquisitions of human capital are major contributions to economic modernization. It is an income-increasing process. Increases in income, extensions of markets, and additional specialization interact. Each has a positive effect on the others. These effects are the basic sources of the self-sustaining properties of economic modernization. Disequilibria are found to be inevitable as modernization is being attained. Economic disorder would increase and dominate were it not for entrepreneurs – individuals and families – restoring economic equilibrium.[20]

Notes and References

1   Zvi Griliches, "Research Costs and Social Returns: Hybrid Corn and Related Innovations," *Journal of Political Economics* 66, October 1958, 419–31; "Hybrid Corn: An Explora-

tion in Economics of Technological Change," *Econometrica*, 1957; and *Technology, Education and Productivity*, Basil Blackwell, New York and Oxford, 1988. The unifying thread that runs through Griliches' papers is the view that technological change is itself an economic phenomenon.

2 Robert E. Lucas, Jr, "On the Mechanics of Economic Development," his Marshall Lecture (Cambridge University, May 1985), *Journal of Monetary Economics*, 22, 1988, 3–42.

3 Fritz Machlup, *The Production and Distribution of Knowledge in the United States*, Princeton University Press, Princeton, NJ, 1962; *Knowledge: Its Creation, Distribution, and Economic Significance. Knowledge and Knowledge Productivity*, Princeton University Press, Princeton, NJ, 1980; *The Branches of Learning*, Princeton University Press, Princeton, NJ, 1982; and his last *The Economics of Information and Human Capital*, Princeton University Press, Princeton, NJ, 1984.

4 Gary S. Becker, "Human Capital, Effort, and the Sexual Division of Labor," *Journal of Labor Economics*, 3 (1), 1985, 533–58.

5 Sherwin Rosen, "Substitution and Division of Labor," *Econometrica*, 45 (1), 1976, 861–8. Also, "Specialization and Human Capital," *Journal of Labor Economics*, 1, 1983, 43–9.

6 Allyn A. Young, "Increasing Returns and Economic Progress," *Economic Journal*, December 1928, 527–42.

7 Alfred Marshall, *Principles of Economics*, 8th edn, Macmillan, London, October 1920, Book IV, ch. xiii, p. 318.

8 Frank H. Knight, *Risk, Uncertainty and Profit*, in the preface of the reissue, the London School of Economics and Political Science, University of London, reprinted 1933, p. xxiii.

9 Kenneth E. Boulding, *Economic Analysis*, revised edition, Harper and Brothers, New York, 1948, ch. 30, p. 637.

10 John Hicks, *Capital and Growth*, Oxford University Press, Oxford, 1965, ch. II, pp. 18–19.

11 Gary S. Becker, *Economic Theory*, Knopf, New York, 1971, p. 123. In a footnote, all too brief, Becker is explicit on this point.

12 Ibid., p. 113.

13 D. P. Chaudhri, "Education and Agricultural Productivity in India," Ph.D. Dissertation, University of Delhi, 1968.

14 Finis Welch, "Education in Production," *Journal of Political Economy*, 78, January–February 1970, 35–9; and "The Role of Investment in Human Capital in Agriculture," in *Distortions of Agricultural Incentives*, edited by Theodore W. Schultz, Indiana University Press, Bloomington, IN, 1978, pp. 259–81.

15 Zvi Griliches, "The Sources of Measured Productivity Growth: United States Agriculture, 1940–1960," *Journal of Political Economy*, 71, 1963, 331–46; and "Research Expenditures, Education, and the Aggregate Agricultural Production Function," *American Economic Review*, 54, 1964, 961–74.

16 Robert Evenson, "The Contribution of Agricultural Research and Extension to Agricultural Production," Ph.D. Dissertation, University of Chicago, 1968.

17 Wallace E. Huffman, "Contributions of Education and Extension in Differential Rates of Change," Ph.D. Dissertation, University of Chicago, 1972; "Decision Making; The Role of Education," *American Journal of Agricultural Economics*, 56, 1974, 85–97; and "Allocative Efficiency: The Role of Human Capital," *Quarterly Journal of Economics*, 91, 1977, 59–77. Huffman focused on the use of a single input, nitrogen fertilizer, in the production of corn. He reasoned that, where a major economic change occurs with various lesser changes in its wake, the education of farmers should increase the rate of the adjustments. His major economic change was the 22–25 percent decline in the price of nitrogen relative to that of corn. Using a sample of county data drawn from five key corn belt states for the period from 1950–4 to 1964, he found that one additional year of schooling resulted in farmers earning $52 more from this one dimension of improved allocative efficiency in one farm activity, that is, in using nitrogen in corn production.

18 Todd E. Petzel, "Education and the Dynamics of Supply," Ph.D. Dissertation, University of Chicago, 1976.

19 Dean T. Jamison and Lawrence J. Lau, *Farmer Education and Farm Efficiency*, Johns Hopkins University Press, Baltimore, MD, 1982, ix and 292 pages.

20 John M. Letiche urged me to write this closing chapter. He had read the paper that I presented at the Buffalo Conference on Human Capital and Economic Growth. He felt it would serve

me in summary. Professor Letiche also read the entire manuscript and made many helpful suggestions for which I am indebted to him.

Index